PASTA
BEST-EVER PASTA & SAUCE RECIPES

PASTA
BEST-EVER PASTA & SAUCE RECIPES

bay books

MEAL PLANNER

Use the following table to plan your best-ever Pasta meal. The recipes have been grouped into appropriate classifications and the portion size of each recipe is clearly shown. Plan your meal and then turn to the appropriate page to find your clear and concise recipe together with a large-format picture of the finished dish.

VEGETARIAN

Even though there are 300 different shapes available today, there is nothing very complicated about pasta; it is one of the simplest foods to cook and also one of the most versatile. Nevertheless, here are a few tips on how best to prepare and serve pasta, and even instructions for making your own.

FRESH OR DRIED?

Basic dried pasta is made with durum wheat semolina and water, which is passed through a die to make shaped pastas or long pasta such as spaghetti. In the recipes in this book, when the ingredient list simply states 'pasta' we are referring to dried pasta.

Fresh pasta is made either with a soft wheat or durum wheat semolina and water. When fresh pasta is more appropriate to a recipe we will state 'fresh pasta' in the ingredient list.

Many people assume that fresh pasta must be 'better' than dried. This is not the case—some sauces are better teamed with fresh pasta and some are best with dried. Fresh pasta works well with rich sauces made from cream, butter and cheese, because its soft texture absorbs the sauce. Alfredo is one of the nicest sauces to serve on fresh pasta, as is plain butter and Parmesan. Dried pasta is more robust if you're serving a hearty tomato-based sauce. If your sauce has olives, anchovies, chillies, meat or seafood, you'll almost certainly be better using dried pasta.

STORING PASTA

Dried pasta can be stored in a cool dry place for months. However, dried wholewheat pasta will only last for one month before turning rancid. Fresh pasta must be refrigerated and won't keep for as long, so buy it as you need it. Filled pasta is best bought a day or so before you need it, but some vacuum-packed filled pastas can be kept for up to three weeks (check the use-by date). It can also be frozen in a single layer between sheets of plastic wrap for up to three months but creamy fillings don't freeze well.

MATCHING THE SAUCE TO THE PASTA

With up to 300 different pasta shapes, it can be confusing knowing which sauce to serve with which pasta. A basic rule to remember is that a chunky pasta is best with a chunky sauce and a thin pasta is best with a thin sauce. Chunky pasta shapes enable you to pick up the sauce with the pasta. Smooth, slender pasta shapes will not hold a chunky sauce but will suit an olive oil or fresh tomato sauce. Tubular shapes such as penne capture thick sauces, while flat or long pastas are traditionally served with thin smooth sauces. Some pastas are ridged specifically so that they can capture more sauce. Tiny pasta such as ditalini or stelline are usually smooth and used in soups; larger pastas would absorb too much of the liquid. Many of the different pasta shapes are shown over the following pages.

HOW MUCH PASTA?

Pasta varies so much in shape, size and type, it is hard to be specific about how much pasta you need per serve. As a general guide, use about 90 g (3 oz) of dried pasta per person for a starter and 150 g (5 oz) for a main course. With fresh pasta (which weighs a little more because it contains more water) use approximately 60 g (2 oz) for a starter and 125 g (4 oz) for a main course.

How much sauce is obviously a matter of personal taste, but it should be pointed out that in Italy pasta is served with only enough sauce to just coat the pasta. Once the pasta and sauce are tossed together, there should be no sauce left sitting in the bottom of the bowl.

COOKING PASTA

Pasta should be cooked in a large deep saucepan of water to prevent the pasta pieces from sticking to each other. Allow about 6 litres (24 cups) of water for every 500 g (1 lb) pasta, but never use less than 4 litres (16 cups) even for a small amount of pasta. Filled pasta and large pasta such as lasagne will need more water, between 9 litres (36 cups) and 12 litres (48 cups), because they are more likely to stick.

If you need to cook large amounts of pasta, only cook up to 1 kg (2 lb) in one saucepan.

Always bring the water to the boil before adding salt (purely to add flavour and a matter of personal preference) and then stirring in the pasta. When the water comes back to the boil, begin timing, stirring often once the pasta softens a little. Test the pasta just prior to the final cooking time on the packet.

Fresh pasta from a delicatessen or pasta shop usually only needs 1–2 minutes. Vacuum-packed fresh pasta from the supermarket requires a little longer—about 6 minutes. Dried pasta varies depending on the size and shape but, because it needs rehydrating as well as cooking, it usually takes longer than fresh pasta. For the most accurate times for all pasta, follow the instructions on the packet.

The best way to ensure pasta is cooked is to taste it. The pasta should be just tender and still retain a slight bite—this is referred to in Italian as *al dente* which literally means 'to the tooth'.

Adding oil to the cooking water contributes very little and can make the pasta too slippery to hold sauce.

Feed the pasta through the rollers on the widest setting. Repeat this three times.

Attach the cutting blades to the machine, the wide for tagliatelle and the narrow for linguine.

Feed a sheet of pasta into the machine and collect the pasta as it comes out of the end.

Either hang the pasta up to dry or coil it into nests and toss with semolina.

Once the pasta is cooked, it is important to drain it in a colander and then turn it either back into the cooking pan to keep warm, into a heated dish or into a pan or dish with the sauce.

Don't overdrain the pasta: it needs to be a little wet for the sauce to coat it well. Never leave pasta sitting in the colander or it will clump together. If you have mistimed your cooking and the sauce isn't ready, put the pasta back into the hot pan and toss with a small amount of olive oil or butter to prevent it from sticking together. Alternatively, lightly spray the drained pasta with some boiling water and toss it gently (it is always a good idea to keep a little of the cooking water for this, in case you overdrain).

MAKING YOUR OWN PASTA

To make pasta to serve four as a main course, you will need 300 g (10 oz) of plain flour, 3 large (60 g/2 oz) eggs, 30 ml (1 fl oz) of olive oil, optional, and a pinch of salt.

All the ingredients should be brought to room temperature before you start. The proportion of flour to eggs depends on the weather, the quality of the flour and the age and size of the eggs.

Use plain or unbleached flour, which gives a well-textured, light dough with good manageability. A percentage of durum wheat semolina is favoured by some pasta makers as it improves flavour, colour and texture. However, its hard-wheat qualities sometimes make it difficult to work, particularly on a hand-cranked machine and any proportion greater than equal parts durum wheat semolina to plain flour can cause problems.

To mix the dough by hand, mound the plain flour on a work surface or in a bowl and make a well in the centre.

Break the eggs into the well and add the oil, if using, and a large pinch of salt. Begin to whisk the eggs and oil together with a fork, incorporating a little of the flour as you do so.

Gradually blend the flour with the eggs, working from the centre out. Use your free hand to hold the mound in place and stop leakage if any of the egg escapes.

Knead the dough on a lightly floured surface with smooth, light strokes, turning it as you fold and press. It should be soft and pliable, but dry to the touch. If it is sticky, knead in a little flour.

It will take at least 6 minutes kneading to achieve a smooth and elastic texture with a slightly glossy appearance. If durum wheat semolina is used, the kneading will take a little longer, at least 8 minutes. Put the dough in a plastic bag without sealing, or cover with a tea towel or an upturned bowl. Allow to rest for 30 minutes.

ROLLING AND CUTTING

Divide the dough into three or four manageable portions and cover with plastic wrap to prevent drying out.

Dust the work surface with semolina (flour will make the pasta heavier). Flatten the first piece of dough so that it is easier to roll through the machine.

On the widest setting, feed the dough through the rollers. Fold the flattened dough in half or thirds so it fits across the rollers. Repeat three times to create a velvety texture. As each sheet is completed, place it on a dry tea towel. Leave uncovered to surface dry for 10 minutes if the sheets are to be cut, but cover them if they are to be used for filled pasta.

Attach the cutting blades to your machine, the wide one for tagliatelle and the narrower one for linguine.

Feed a sheet of pasta into the machine and carefully collect the pasta as it comes out the other end.

Either hang up the pasta to dry over a wooden spoon or on a pasta dryer or coil it into nests. To keep the nests from sticking, toss in a little semolina.

INGREDIENTS

Pesto

2 garlic cloves

50 g (1³/₄ oz) pine nuts

120 g (4¹/₂ oz) basil, stems removed

150–180 ml (5–6 fl oz) extra virgin olive oil

50 g (1³/₄ oz) Parmesan cheese, finely grated,
   plus extra to serve

500 g (1 lb 2 oz) trenette

175 g (6 oz) green beans, trimmed

175 g (6 oz) small potatoes, very thinly sliced

1 Put the garlic and pine nuts in a mortar and pestle or food processor and pound or process until finely ground. Add the basil and then drizzle in the olive oil a little at a time while pounding or processing. When you have a thick purée stop adding the oil. Season and mix in the Parmesan.

2 Bring a large saucepan of salted water to the boil. Add the pasta, green beans and potatoes, stirring well to prevent the pasta from sticking together. Cook until the pasta is al dente (the vegetables should be cooked by this time), then drain, reserving a little of the water.

3 Return the pasta and vegetables to the saucepan, add the pesto, and mix well. If necessary, add some of the reserved water to loosen the pasta. Season and serve immediately with the extra Parmesan.

INGREDIENTS

Pesto

2 cloves garlic, crushed

1 teaspoon sea salt

3 tablespoons pine nuts, toasted

2 cups (60 g/2 oz) fresh basil

$^1/_2$ cup (50 g/1$^3/_4$ oz) grated Parmesan

$^1/_3$ cup (80 ml/2$^3/_4$ fl oz) extra virgin olive oil

500 g (1 lb) orecchiette or shell pasta

2 tablespoons olive oil

150 g (5 oz) jar capers, drained and patted dry

2 tablespoons extra virgin olive oil

2 cloves garlic, chopped

3 tomatoes, seeded and diced

300 g (10 oz) thin asparagus spears, cut in half and blanched

2 tablespoons balsamic vinegar

200 g (6$^1/_2$ oz) rocket, trimmed and cut into short lengths

Parmesan shavings, to garnish

1   To make the pesto, place the garlic, sea salt and pine nuts in a food processor or blender and process until combined. Add the basil and Parmesan and process until finely minced. With the motor running, add the oil in a thin steady stream and blend until smooth.

2   Cook the pasta in a large saucepan of boiling water until al dente, then drain well.

3   Meanwhile, heat the oil in a frying pan, add the capers and fry over high heat, stirring occasionally, for 4–5 minutes, or until crisp. Remove from the pan and drain on crumpled paper towels.

4   In the same frying pan, heat the extra virgin olive oil over medium heat and add the garlic, tomato and asparagus. Cook for 1–2 minutes, or until warmed through, tossing well. Stir in the balsamic vinegar.

5   Drain the pasta and transfer to a large serving bowl. Add the pesto and toss, coating the pasta well. Cool slightly. Add the tomato mixture and rocket and season to taste with salt and cracked black pepper. Toss well and sprinkle with the capers and Parmesan. Serve warm.

INGREDIENTS

100 g (3½ oz) button mushrooms
1 large yellow capsicum
1 large red capsicum
cooking oil spray
100 g (3½ oz) lean fillet steak
1½ cups (135 g/4½ oz) penne

Pesto
1 cup (50 g/1¾ oz) tightly packed basil leaves
2 cloves garlic, chopped
2 tablespoons pepitas (pumpkin seeds)
1 tablespoon olive oil
2 tablespoons orange juice
1 tablespoon lemon juice

1 Cut the mushrooms into quarters. Cut the capsicums into large flat pieces, removing the seeds and membrane. Place skin-side-up under a hot grill until blackened. Leave covered with a tea towel until cool, then peel away the skin and chop the flesh.

2 Spray a non-stick frying pan with oil and cook the steak over high heat for 3–4 minutes each side until it is medium-rare. Remove and leave for 5 minutes before cutting into thin slices. Season with a little salt.

3 To make the pesto, finely chop the basil leaves, garlic and pepitas in a food processor. With the motor running, add the oil, orange and lemon juice. Season well.

4 Meanwhile, cook the penne in a large pan of rapidly boiling salted water until al dente. Drain, then toss with the pesto in a large bowl.

5 Add the capsicum pieces, steak slices and mushroom quarters to the penne and toss to distribute evenly. Serve immediately.

INGREDIENTS

300 g (10 oz) plain (all-purpose) flour
3 eggs, beaten
3 tablespoons oil
1 cup (250 g/8 oz) ricotta cheese
2 tablespoons grated Parmesan
2 teaspoons chopped fresh chives
1 tablespoon chopped flat-leaf parsley
2 teaspoons chopped fresh basil
1 teaspoon chopped fresh lemon thyme or thyme
1 egg, beaten, extra

1   Sift the flour into a bowl and make a well in the centre. Gradually mix in the eggs and oil.
    Turn out onto a lightly floured surface and knead for 6 minutes, or until smooth. Cover with
    plastic wrap and leave for 30 minutes.

2   To make the filling, mix the ricotta, Parmesan and herbs. Season well.

3   Divide the dough into four portions and shape each into a log. Keeping the unworked
    portions covered, take one portion and flatten it with one or two rolls of a rolling pin. With
    machine rollers set to the widest setting, crank the dough through two or three times. Fold
    it into thirds, turn the dough by 90 degrees and feed it through again. If the dough feels
    sticky, flour it lightly each time it is rolled. Repeat the rolling and folding 8–10 times until
    the dough feels smooth and elastic. Reduce the width of the rollers by one setting and
    pass the dough through without folding it. Repeat, setting the rollers one notch closer
    each time until you have reached a thickness of 2 mm ($^1/_6$ inch). Roll another sheet
    slightly larger than the first and cover with a tea towel.

4   Spread the smaller sheet out onto a work surface. Spoon 1 teaspoon of the filling at 5 cm
    (2 inch) intervals. Brush the beaten egg between the filling along the cutting lines. Place
    the larger sheet on top. Press the two sheets together along the cutting line. Cut the
    ravioli with a pastry wheel or knife. Transfer to a lightly floured baking tray. Repeat with the
    remaining dough and filling. Can be stored in the refrigerator for 1–2 days.

5   Cook the ravioli in a large pan of salted boiling water for 5–8 minutes and top with a
    sauce of your choice.

WARM PESTO AND PRAWN SALAD

INGREDIENTS

Pesto
2 cloves garlic, crushed
1 teaspoon salt
¼ cup (40 g/1¼ oz) pine nuts, toasted
2 cups (60 g/2 oz) fresh basil
½ cup (60 g/2 oz) grated Parmesan
¼ cup (60 ml/2 fl oz) extra virgin olive oil

500 g (1 lb) pasta
150 g (5 oz) jar capers in brine
3 tablespoons olive oil
2 tablespoons extra virgin olive oil
2 cloves garlic, chopped
2 tomatoes, seeded and diced
150 g (5 oz) thin asparagus, trimmed, halved and blanched
2 tablespoons balsamic vinegar
150 g (5 oz) rocket
20 cooked prawns, peeled, tails intact
shaved Parmesan, to garnish

1 For the pesto, blend the garlic, salt, pine nuts, fresh basil leaves and grated Parmesan in a food processor or blender until thoroughly combined. With the motor running, add the oil in a thin steady stream and process until the pesto is smooth.

2 Cook the pasta in a large pan of rapidly boiling salted water until al dente. Drain well, transfer to a large bowl and toss the pesto through.

3 Pat the drained capers dry with paper towels, then heat the olive oil in a frying pan and fry the capers for 4–5 minutes, stirring occasionally, until crisp. Drain on paper towels.

4 Heat the extra virgin olive oil in a deep frying pan over medium heat and add the garlic, tomatoes and asparagus. Toss continuously for 1–2 minutes, or until warmed through. Stir in the balsamic vinegar.

5 When the pasta is just warm, not hot (or it will wilt the rocket), toss the tomato mixture, rocket and prawns with the pasta and season with salt and pepper, to taste. Serve sprinkled with capers and shaved Parmesan.

INGREDIENTS

200 g (6¹/₂ oz) dried borlotti beans
¹/₄ cup (60 ml/2 fl oz) olive oil
90 g (3 oz) piece pancetta, finely diced
1 onion, finely chopped
2 cloves garlic, crushed
1 celery stick, thinly sliced
1 carrot, diced
1 bay leaf
1 sprig fresh rosemary
1 sprig fresh flat-leaf parsley
400 g (13 oz) can diced tomatoes, drained
1.6 litres vegetable stock
2 tablespoons finely chopped fresh flat-leaf parsley
150 g (5 oz) ditalini or other small dried pasta
extra virgin olive oil, to serve
grated fresh Parmesan, to serve

1   Place the beans in a large bowl, cover with cold water and leave to soak overnight. Drain and rinse.

2   Heat the oil in a large saucepan, add the pancetta, onion, garlic, celery and carrot, and cook over medium heat for 5 minutes, or until golden. Season with pepper. Add the bay leaf, rosemary, parsley, tomato, stock and beans, and bring to the boil. Reduce the heat and simmer for 1¹/₂ hours, or until the beans are tender. Add more boiling water if necessary to maintain the liquid level.

3   Discard the bay leaf, rosemary and parsley sprigs. Scoop out 1 cup (250 ml/8 fl oz) of the bean mixture and purée in a food processor or blender. Return to the pan, season with salt and ground black pepper, and add the parsley and pasta. Simmer for 6 minutes, or until the pasta is al dente. Remove from the heat and set aside for 10 minutes. Serve drizzled with extra virgin olive oil and sprinkled with Parmesan.

NOTE   If you prefer, you can use three 400 g (13 oz) cans drained borlotti beans. Simmer with the other vegetables for 30 minutes.

INGREDIENTS

125 g (4 oz) dried borlotti beans
1 large onion, roughly chopped
2 cloves garlic
$^1/_4$ cup (7 g/$^1/_4$ oz) roughly chopped fresh flat-leaf parsley
60 g (2 oz) pancetta, chopped
1/4 cup (60 ml/2 fl oz) olive oil
1 celery stick, halved lengthways, cut into 1 cm ($^1/_2$ inch)
   slices
1 carrot, halved lengthways, cut into 1 cm ($^1/_2$ inch) slices
1 potato, diced
2 teaspoons tomato paste
400 g (13 oz) can diced tomatoes
6 fresh basil leaves, roughly torn
2 litres chicken or vegetable stock
2 thin zucchini, cut into 1.5 cm ($^5/_8$ inch) slices
$^3/_4$ cup (115 g/4 oz) shelled peas
60 g (2 oz) green beans, cut into 4 cm (1$^1/_2$ inch) lengths
80 g (2$^3/_4$ oz) silverbeet leaves, shredded
75 g (2$^1/_2$ oz) ditalini or small pasta

Pesto
1 cup (30 g/1 oz) loosely packed fresh basil leaves
20 g ($^3/_4$ oz) lightly toasted pine nuts
2 cloves garlic
100 ml (3$^1/_2$ fl oz) olive oil
$^1/_4$ cup (25 g/$^3/_4$ oz) grated fresh Parmesan

1 Put the beans in a large bowl, cover with water and soak overnight. Drain and rinse under cold water.

2 Place the onion, garlic, parsley and pancetta in a food processor and process until finely chopped. Heat the oil in a saucepan, add the pancetta mixture and cook over low heat, stirring occasionally, for 8–10 minutes.

3 Add the celery, carrot and potato, and cook for 5 minutes, then stir in the tomato paste, tomato, basil and borlotti beans. Season with black pepper. Add the stock and bring slowly to the boil. Cover and simmer, stirring occasionally, for 1$^1/_2$ hours.

4 Season, and add the zucchini, peas, green beans, silverbeet and pasta. Simmer for 8–10 minutes, or until the vegetables and pasta are al dente.

5 To make the pesto, combine the basil, pine nuts and garlic with a pinch of salt in a food processor. Process until finely chopped. With the motor running, slowly add the olive oil. Transfer to a bowl and stir in the Parmesan and ground black pepper to taste. Serve the soup in bowls with the pesto on top.

INGREDIENTS

1 cup (250 ml/8 fl oz) olive oil
2 bird's eye chillies, seeded and thinly sliced
5–6 large cloves garlic, crushed
500 g (1 lb) spaghetti
100 g (3¹/₂ oz) thinly sliced prosciutto
¹/₂ cup (30 g/1 oz) chopped fresh flat-leaf parsley
2 tablespoons chopped fresh basil
2 tablespoons chopped fresh oregano
³/₄ cup (75 g/2¹/₂ oz) grated Parmesan

1 Pour the oil into a small saucepan with the chilli and garlic. Slowly heat the oil over low heat for about 12 minutes to infuse the oil with the garlic and chilli. Don't allow the oil to reach smoking point or the garlic will burn and taste bitter.

2 Meanwhile, cook the pasta in a large pan of rapidly boiling salted water until al dente. Drain well and return to the pan to keep warm. Cook the prosciutto under a hot grill for 2 minutes each side, or until crispy. Cool and break into pieces.

3 Pour the hot oil mixture over the spaghetti and toss well with the prosciutto, fresh herbs and Parmesan. Season to taste.

NOTE This sauce is traditionally served with spaghetti. It is simple but relies on good-quality ingredients.

SPAGHETTI WITH HERB, GARLIC AND CHILLI OIL

SPINACH AND RICOTTA GNOCCHI

INGREDIENTS

4 slices white bread
½ cup (125 ml/4 fl oz) milk
500 g (1 lb) frozen spinach, thawed
250 g (8 oz) ricotta cheese
2 eggs
60 g (2 oz) Parmesan, grated
¼ cup (30 g/1 oz) plain flour
Parmesan shavings, to serve

Garlic butter sauce
100 g (3½ oz) butter
2 cloves garlic, crushed
3 tablespoons chopped fresh basil
1 ripe tomato, diced

1 Remove the crusts from the bread and soak in milk in a shallow dish for 10 minutes. Squeeze out any excess milk from the bread. Squeeze out any excess liquid from the spinach.

2 Place the bread, spinach, ricotta, eggs and Parmesan in a bowl and mix thoroughly. Refrigerate, covered, for 1 hour. Fold the flour in well.

3 Lightly dust your hands in flour and roll heaped teaspoons of the mixture into dumplings. Lower batches of the gnocchi into a large saucepan of boiling salted water. Cook for about 2 minutes, or until the gnocchi rise to the surface. Transfer to a serving plate and keep warm.

4 To make the sauce, combine all the ingredients in a small saucepan and cook over medium heat for 3 minutes, or until the butter is nutty brown. Drizzle over the gnocchi and sprinkle with the shaved Parmesan.

INGREDIENTS

2 tablespoons olive oil
1 large onion, finely chopped
2 celery sticks, finely chopped
3 vine-ripened tomatoes
1.5 litres chicken or vegetable stock
½ cup (90 g/3 oz) ditalini pasta
2 tablespoons chopped fresh flat-leaf parsley

1   Heat the oil in a large saucepan over medium heat. Add the onion and celery and cook for 5 minutes, or until they have softened.

2   Score a cross in the base of each tomato, then place them in a bowl of boiling water for 1 minute. Plunge into cold water and peel the skin away from the cross. Halve the tomatoes and scoop out the seeds. Roughly chop the flesh. Add the stock and tomato to the onion mixture and bring to the boil. Add the pasta and cook for 10 minutes, or until al dente. Season and sprinkle with parsley. Serve with crusty bread.

INGREDIENTS

1 tablespoon olive oil
1 onion, finely chopped
3 cloves garlic, crushed
2 x 300 g (10 oz) cans mixed beans, drained
1.75 litres chicken stock (see note)
100 g (3¹/₂ oz) conchigliette
1 tablespoon chopped fresh tarragon

1 Heat the oil in a saucepan over low heat. Add the onion and cook for 5 minutes, then add the garlic and cook for a further 1 minute, stirring frequently. Add the beans and chicken stock and then cover the pan with a lid.

2 Increase the heat and bring to the boil. Add the pasta and cook until al dente. Stir in the tarragon, then season with salt and cracked black pepper. Serve with crusty bread.

NOTE The flavour of this soup is really enhanced by using a good-quality stock. Either make your own or use the tetra packs of liquid stock that are available at the supermarket.

INGREDIENTS

150 g (5¹/₂ oz) spaghetti, broken into 8 cm (3 inch) lengths
1.5 litres (6 cups) beef stock
3 teaspoons tomato paste (purée)
400 g (14 oz) can chopped tomatoes
3 tablespoons basil leaves, torn
shaved Parmesan cheese, to garnish

Meatballs
1 tablespoon oil
1 onion, finely chopped
2 garlic cloves, crushed
500 g (1 lb 2 oz) lean minced (ground) beef
3 tablespoons finely chopped flat-leaf (Italian) parsley
3 tablespoons fresh breadcrumbs
2 tablespoons finely grated Parmesan cheese
1 egg, lightly beaten

1   Cook the spaghetti in a large saucepan of boiling water according to packet instructions until al dente. Drain. Put the stock and 500 ml (2 cups) water in a large saucepan and slowly bring to a simmer.

2   Meanwhile, to make the meatballs, heat the oil in a small frying pan over medium heat and cook the onion for 2–3 minutes, or until soft. Add the garlic and cook for 30 seconds. Allow to cool.

3   Combine the mince, parsley, breadcrumbs, Parmesan, egg, the onion mixture, and salt and pepper. Roll a heaped teaspoon of mixture into a ball, making 40 balls in total.

4   Stir the tomato paste and tomato into the beef stock and simmer for 2–3 minutes. Drop in the meatballs, return to a simmer and cook for 10 minutes, or until cooked through. Stir in the spaghetti and basil to warm through. Season, garnish with shaved Parmesan and serve.

ITALIAN OMELETTE

2 tablespoons olive oil
1 onion, finely chopped
125 g (4 oz) ham, sliced
6 eggs
3 tablespoons milk
2 cups (350 g/11 oz) cooked fusilli or spiral pasta (see note)
¼ cup (25 g/¾ oz) grated Parmesan
2 tablespoons chopped fresh parsley
1 tablespoon chopped fresh basil
½ cup (60 g/2 oz) grated Cheddar

1 Heat half the oil in pan. Add the onion and stir over low heat until tender. Add the ham and stir for 1 minute. Transfer to a plate.

2 Whisk together the eggs, milk, salt and pepper. Stir in the pasta, Parmesan, herbs and onion mixture.

3 Preheat the grill to hot. Heat the remaining oil in the same pan. Pour the egg mixture into the pan. Sprinkle with Cheddar. Cook over medium heat until the omelette begins to set around the edges then place under the grill until lightly browned on top. Cut into wedges for serving.

NOTE To get 2 cups of cooked pasta you will need to start with about 150 g (5 oz) of uncooked dried pasta.

INGREDIENTS

200 g (6½ oz) spiral pasta

425 g (14 oz) can cream of mushroom or broccoli soup

1 cup (250 g/8 oz) sour cream

1 teaspoon curry powder

1 barbecued chicken

250 g (8 oz) broccoli, cut into small pieces

1 cup (80 g/2¾ oz) fresh breadcrumbs

1½ cups (185 g/6 oz) grated Cheddar

1   Preheat the oven to moderate 180°C (350°F/Gas 4). Bring a saucepan of salted water to the boil, add the pasta and cook for 10–12 minutes, or until al dente. Drain.

2   Combine the soup, sour cream and curry powder, and season with freshly ground black pepper.

3   Remove the meat from the chicken. Discard the carcass and roughly chop the chicken. Combine the chicken with the cooked pasta, broccoli and soup mixture. Spoon the mixture into four lightly greased 2 cup (500 ml/16 fl oz) ovenproof dishes, and sprinkle with the combined breadcrumbs and grated cheese. Bake for 25–30 minutes, or until the cheese melts.

INGREDIENTS

500 g (1 lb) orange sweet potato, cut into large pieces
$^1/_4$ cup (60 ml/2 fl oz) olive oil
150 g (5 oz) ricotta cheese
1 tablespoon chopped fresh basil
1 clove garlic, crushed
2 tablespoons grated Parmesan
2 x 250 g (8 oz) packets egg won ton wrappers
60 g (2 oz) butter
4 spring onions, sliced on the diagonal
2 cloves garlic, crushed, extra
300 ml (10 fl oz) cream
baby basil leaves, to serve

1 Preheat the oven to hot 220°C (425°F/Gas 7). Place the sweet potato on a baking tray and drizzle with oil. Bake for 40 minutes, or until tender.

2 Transfer the sweet potato to a bowl with the ricotta, basil, garlic and Parmesan and mash until smooth.

3 Cover the won ton wrappers with a damp tea towel. Place 2 level teaspoons of the sweet potato mixture into the centre of one wrapper and brush the edges with a little water. Top with another wrapper. Place onto a baking tray lined with baking paper and cover with a tea towel. Repeat with the remaining ingredients to make 60 ravioli, placing a sheet of baking paper between each layer.

4 Melt the butter in a frying pan. Add the spring onion and garlic and cook over medium heat for 1 minute. Add the cream, bring to the boil, then reduce the heat and simmer for 4–5 minutes, or until the cream has reduced and thickened. Keep warm.

5 Bring a large saucepan of water to the boil. Cook the ravioli in batches for 2–4 minutes, or until just tender. Drain well. Ladle the hot sauce over the top of the ravioli, garnish with the basil leaves and serve immediately.

INGREDIENTS

1.5 kg (3 lb) vine-ripened tomatoes
2 cloves garlic, crushed
1 teaspoon sugar
$^1/_3$ cup (80 ml/2$^3/_4$ fl oz) olive oil
3 tablespoons chopped fresh flat-leaf parsley
6 fresh lasagne sheets
400 g (13 oz) smoked salmon
100 g (3$^1/_2$ oz) baby rocket leaves
extra virgin olive oil, for drizzling

1 Score a cross in the base of each tomato and place in a bowl of boiling water for 1 minute. Plunge into cold water and peel the skin away from the cross. Remove the core, then transfer to a food processor or blender and, using the pulse button, process until roughly chopped. Transfer to a saucepan with the garlic and sugar, bring to the boil, then reduce the heat and simmer for 5 minutes, or until reduced slightly. Remove from the heat and gradually whisk in the oil. Stir in the parsley and season. Keep warm.

2 Cut the lasagne sheets in half widthways to give 12 pieces, each about 12 cm (5 inches) squares. Cook the pasta in a large saucepan of boiling water in two batches until al dente. Remove from the water and lay out flat to prevent sticking.

3 Place a pasta sheet on each of four plates. Set aside $^1/_3$ cup of the tomato mix. Spoon half the remaining tomato mixture over the pasta sheets, then half the smoked salmon and rocket leaves. Repeat to give two layers. Finish with a third sheet of pasta.

4 Top each pasta stack with a tablespoon of the tomato sauce, drizzle with a little extra virgin olive oil and serve immediately.

INGREDIENTS

250 g (8 oz) chicken breast fillet
$1^1/_2$ cups (375 ml/12 fl oz) chicken stock
350 g (11 oz) fusilli pasta
155 g (5 oz) asparagus, cut into short lengths
150 g (5 oz) Gruyère cheese, grated
2 spring onions, thinly sliced

Dressing
$^1/_4$ cup (60 ml/2 fl oz) olive oil
$^1/_4$ cup (60 ml/2 fl oz) lemon juice
$^1/_2$ teaspoon sugar

1 Put the chicken and stock in a frying pan. Bring to the boil, then reduce the heat and poach gently, turning regularly, for 8 minutes, or until tender. Remove the chicken, cool and slice thinly.

2 Cook the pasta in a large pan of boiling salted water for 10–12 minutes, or until al dente. Drain and cool.

3 Cook the asparagus in boiling water for 2 minutes. Drain and place in a bowl of iced water. Drain again. Combine with the chicken, pasta and cheese in a large bowl.

4 To make the dressing, whisk the ingredients together. Season with salt and pepper. Add to the salad and toss well. Transfer to a serving bowl and scatter with the spring onion.

125 g (4 oz) day-old crusty bread, crusts removed

1^1/$_2$ cups (185 g/6 oz) walnut pieces

500 g (1 lb) pasta shells

^{1}/$_2$ cup (30 g/1 oz) firmly packed fresh basil, roughly chopped

2–3 cloves garlic, peeled

1 small fresh red chilli, seeded and roughly chopped

^{1}/$_2$ teaspoon finely grated lemon rind

^{1}/$_4$ cup (60 ml/2 fl oz) lemon juice

^{1}/$_2$ cup (125 ml/4 fl oz) olive oil

1 Preheat the oven to warm 160°C (315°F/Gas 2–3). Cut the bread into 2 cm (^{3}/$_4$ inch) thick slices and place on a baking tray with the walnuts. Bake for 8–10 minutes, or until the bread is dried out a little and the walnuts are lightly toasted. Don't overcook the walnuts or they will become bitter.

2 Meanwhile, cook the pasta in a large pan of rapidly boiling salted water until al dente. Drain and return to the pan to keep warm.

3 Break the bread into chunks and mix in a food processor with the walnuts, basil, garlic, chilli, lemon rind and juice. Use the pulse button to chop the mixture without forming a paste. Transfer to a bowl and stir in the oil. Toss through the pasta, then season to taste with salt and pepper.

PASTA SHELLS WITH WALNUT PESTO

COTELLI WITH CAPERS, BOCCONCINI AND BASIL OIL

$1/2$ cup (125 ml/4 fl oz) olive oil

125 g (4 oz) jar capers in brine, drained

500 g (1 lb) cotelli

2 tablespoons lemon juice

2 cups (100 g/$3^1/2$ oz) firmly packed fresh basil

$1/3$ cup (35 g/1 oz) grated Parmesan

250 g (8 oz) cherry tomatoes, quartered

8 bocconcini, quartered

extra virgin olive oil, for serving

1   Heat half the olive oil in a pan, add the capers and cook over high heat for 3–4 minutes, or until crisp and golden. Drain on paper towels and set aside.

2   Cook the pasta in a large pan of rapidly boiling salted water until al dente. Drain and return to the pan to keep warm. Meanwhile, mix the lemon juice, $1^1/2$ cups (75 g/$2^1/2$ oz) of the basil and the remaining olive oil in a food processor until smooth. Season.

3   Roughly tear the remaining basil leaves, then toss through the warm pasta with the basil mixture, 2 tablespoons of the Parmesan and the cherry tomatoes. Spoon into warmed bowls and top with the bocconcini and capers. Drizzle with extra virgin olive oil and garnish with the remaining grated Parmesan. Serve immediately.

450 g (1 lb) elbow macaroni
40 g (1$^1/_2$ oz) butter
300 ml (10$^1/_2$ fl oz) cream
125 g (4$^1/_2$ oz) fontina cheese, sliced
125 g (4$^1/_2$ oz) provolone cheese, grated
100 g (3$^1/_2$ oz) Gruyère cheese, grated
125 g (4$^1/_2$ oz) blue castello cheese, crumbled
40 g ($^1/_2$ cup) fresh white breadcrumbs
25 g ($^1/_4$ cup) grated Parmesan cheese

1 Preheat the oven to 180°C (350°F/Gas 4). Cook the pasta in a large saucepan of boiling salted water until al dente. Drain and keep warm.

2 Melt half the butter in a large saucepan. Add the cream and, when just coming to the boil, add the fontina, provolone, Gruyère and blue castello cheeses, stirring constantly over low heat for 3 minutes, or until melted. Season with salt and ground white pepper. Add the pasta to the cheese mixture and mix well.

3 Spoon the mixture into a greased shallow 2 litre (8 cup) ovenproof dish. Sprinkle with the breadcrumbs mixed with the Parmesan, dot with the remaining cubed butter and bake for 25 minutes, or until the top is golden and crisp. Serve with a salad.

RICH CHEESE MACARONI

INGREDIENTS

375 g (13 oz) lasagnette
100 g (1 cup) walnuts
40 g (1¹/₂ oz) butter
3 French shallots, finely chopped
1 tablespoon brandy or cognac
250 ml (1 cup) crème fraîche
200 g (7 oz) gorgonzola cheese, crumbled (see note)
70 g (2¹/₂ oz) baby English spinach leaves

1 Preheat the oven to 200°C (400°F/Gas 6). Cook the pasta in a large saucepan of boiling salted water until al dente. Drain, return to the pan and keep warm.

2 Meanwhile, place the walnuts on a baking tray and roast for 5 minutes, or until golden and toasted. Cool, then roughly chop.

3 Heat the butter in a large saucepan, add the shallots and cook over medium heat for 1–2 minutes, or until soft, taking care not to brown. Add the brandy and simmer for 1 minute, then stir in the crème fraîche and gorgonzola. Cook for 3–4 minutes, or until the cheese has melted and the sauce has thickened.

4 Stir in the spinach and toasted walnuts, reserving 1 tablespoon for garnish. Heat gently until the spinach has just wilted. Season with salt and cracked black pepper. Gently mix the sauce through the pasta. Divide among serving plates and sprinkle with the reserved walnuts.

NOTE The gorgonzola needs to be young as this gives a sweeter, milder flavour to the sauce.

INGREDIENTS

2 tablespoons extra virgin olive oil
4 garlic cloves, finely chopped
1 small red chilli, finely chopped
3 x 400 g (14 oz) cans crushed tomatoes
1 teaspoon sugar
80 ml ($^1/_3$ cup) dry white wine
3 tablespoons chopped herbs such as basil or parsley
400 g (14 oz) vermicelli (see note)
35 g ($^1/_3$ cup) shaved Parmesan cheese

1   Heat the oil in a large deep frying pan and cook the garlic and chilli for 1 minute. Add the tomato, sugar, wine, herbs and 440 ml ($1^3/_4$ cups) water. Bring to the boil and season.

2   Reduce the heat to medium and add the pasta, breaking the strands if they are too long. Cook for 10 minutes, or until the pasta is cooked, stirring often to stop the pasta from sticking. The pasta will thicken the sauce as it cooks. Season to taste and serve in bowls with shaved Parmesan.

NOTE   Vermicelli is a pasta similar to spaghetti, but thinner. You can also use spaghettini or angel hair pasta for this recipe.

INGREDIENTS

100 ml extra virgin olive oil
16 thin asparagus spears, cut into 5 cm lengths
375 g spaghettini
120 g rocket, shredded
2 small fresh red chillies, finely chopped
2 teaspoons finely grated lemon rind
1 clove garlic, finely chopped
1 cup (100 g) grated Parmesan
2 tablespoons lemon juice

1   Bring a large saucepan of water to the boil over medium heat. Add 1 tablespoon of the oil and a pinch of salt to the water and blanch the asparagus for 3–4 minutes. Remove the asparagus with a slotted spoon, refresh under cold water, drain and place in a bowl. Return the water to a rapid boil and add the spaghettini. Cook the pasta until al dente. Drain and return to the pan.

2   Meanwhile, add the rocket, chilli, lemon rind, garlic and $^2/_3$ cup (65 g) of the Parmesan to the asparagus and mix well. Add to the pasta, pour on the lemon juice and remaining olive oil and season with salt and freshly ground black pepper. Stir well to evenly coat the pasta with the mixture. Divide among four pasta bowls, top with the remaining Parmesan and serve.

NOTE   You can use other types of pasta such as tagliatelle, macaroni or spiral-shaped pasta.

INGREDIENTS

375 g tagliatelle
140 ml extra virgin olive oil
1 small fresh red chilli, seeded and finely chopped
$1/4$ cup (50 g) drained capers
$1^1/2$ tablespoons fresh lemon thyme leaf tips
500 g tuna steaks, trimmed and cut into 3 cm cubes
$1/4$ cup (60 ml) lemon juice
1 tablespoon grated lemon zest
$1/2$ cup (30 g) chopped fresh flat-leaf parsley

1. Cook the tagliatelle in a large saucepan of rapidly boiling salted water until al dente. Drain, then return to the pan.

2. Meanwhile, heat 1 tablespoon of the oil in a large frying pan. Add the chilli and capers and cook, stirring, for 1 minute, or until the capers are crisp. Add the thyme and cook for another minute. Transfer to a bowl.

3. Heat another tablespoon of oil in the pan. Add the tuna cubes and toss for 2–3 minutes, or until evenly browned on the outside but still pink in the centre—check with the point of a sharp knife. Remove from the heat.

4. Add the tuna to the caper mixture along with the lemon juice, lemon rind, parsley and the remaining oil, stirring gently until combined. Toss through the pasta, season with freshly ground black pepper and serve immediately.

PROSCIUTTO AND SWEET POTATO PENNE

500 g (1 lb) penne
500 g (1 lb) orange sweet potato, diced
2 tablespoons extra virgin olive oil
5 spring onions, sliced
2 small cloves garlic, crushed
8 thin slices prosciutto, chopped
125 g (4 oz) sun-dried tomatoes in oil, drained and sliced
¼ cup (15 g/½ oz) shredded fresh basil leaves

1 Cook the penne in a large pan of rapidly boiling salted water until al dente. Drain well and return to the pan to keep warm.

2 Meanwhile, steam the sweet potato for 5 minutes, or until tender. Heat the oil in a saucepan, add the spring onion, garlic and sweet potato and stir over medium heat for 2–3 minutes, or until the spring onion is soft. Add the prosciutto and tomato and cook for a further 1 minute.

3 Add the sweet potato mixture to the penne and toss over low heat until heated through. Add the basil and season with black pepper. Serve immediately with crusty bread.

NOTE Orange sweet potato is also known as kumera.

INGREDIENTS

Meatballs

500 g (1 lb) beef mince
½ cup (40 g/1¼ oz) fresh breadcrumbs
1 onion, finely chopped
2 cloves garlic, crushed
2 teaspoons Worcestershire sauce
1 teaspoon dried oregano
¼ cup (30 g/1 oz) plain flour
2 tablespoons olive oil

Sauce

2 x 400 g (13 oz) cans chopped tomatoes
1 tablespoon olive oil
1 onion, finely chopped
2 cloves garlic, crushed
2 tablespoons tomato paste
½ cup (125 ml/4 fl oz) beef stock
2 teaspoons sugar

500 g (1 lb) spaghetti
grated Parmesan, to serve

1   Combine the mince, breadcrumbs, onion, garlic, Worcestershire sauce and oregano and season to taste. Use your hands to mix the ingredients well. Roll level tablespoons of the mixture into balls, dust lightly with the flour and shake off the excess. Heat the oil in a deep frying pan and cook the meatballs in batches, turning often, until browned all over. Drain well.

2   To make the sauce, purée the tomatoes in a food processor or blender. Heat the oil in the cleaned frying pan. Add the onion and cook over medium heat for a few minutes until soft and lightly golden. Add the garlic and cook for 1 minute more. Add the puréed tomatoes, tomato paste, stock and sugar to the pan and stir to combine. Bring the mixture to the boil, and add the meatballs. Reduce the heat and simmer for 15 minutes, turning the meatballs once. Season with salt and pepper.

3   Meanwhile, cook the spaghetti in a large pan of boiling water until just tender. Drain, divide among serving plates and top with the meatballs and sauce. Serve with grated Parmesan.

SPAGHETTI WITH MEATBALLS

INGREDIENTS

350 g spaghetti
8 quail eggs (or 4 hen eggs)
3 x 185 g cans tuna in oil
$1/_3$ cup (50 g) pitted and halved Kalamata olives
100 g semi-dried tomatoes, halved lengthways
4 anchovy fillets, chopped into small pieces
1 teaspoon finely grated lemon zest
2 tablespoons lemon juice
3 tablespoons baby capers, drained
3 tablespoons chopped fresh flat-leaf parsley

1   Cook the pasta in a large saucepan of rapidly boiling salted water until al dente.
    Meanwhile, place the eggs in a saucepan of cold water, bring to the boil and cook for
    4 minutes (10 minutes for hen eggs). Drain, cool under cold water, then peel. Cut the quail
    eggs into halves or the hen eggs into quarters.

2   Empty the tuna and its oil into a large bowl. Add the olives, tomato halves, anchovies,
    lemon rind and juice, capers and 2 tablespoons of the parsley. Drain the pasta and rinse in
    a little cold water, then toss gently through the tuna mixture. Divide among serving bowls,
    garnish with egg and the remaining chopped fresh parsley, and serve.

INGREDIENTS

2 tablespoons olive oil

1 teaspoon dried oregano

2 cloves garlic, finely chopped

6 Roma tomatoes, halved

500 g (1 lb) spaghetti

4 slices prosciutto

16 Kalamata olives

200 g (6$\frac{1}{2}$ oz) feta, cut into bite-size cubes

1 tablespoon balsamic vinegar

5 tablespoons olive oil, extra

3 cloves garlic, thinly sliced, extra

60 g (2 oz) rocket leaves, trimmed

1 Preheat the oven to slow 150°C (300°F/Gas 2). Combine the olive oil, oregano, garlic and 1 teaspoon salt in a bowl. Add the tomato and toss to combine, rubbing the mixture onto the cut halves of the tomato. Place the tomato cut-side-up on a lined baking tray and cook in the oven for 1 hour.

2 Meanwhile, cook the pasta in a large pan of rapidly boiling salted water until al dente. Drain well and return to the pan to keep warm. Place the prosciutto on a grill tray and cook under a hot grill, turning once, for 3–4 minutes, or until crispy. Break into pieces.

3 Toss the tomato, olives, feta, spaghetti and balsamic vinegar in a bowl and keep warm.

4 Heat the extra olive oil in a small saucepan and cook the extra garlic over low heat, without burning, for 1–2 minutes, or until the garlic has infused the oil.

5 Pour the garlic and oil over the spaghetti mixture, add the rocket leaves and toss well. Sprinkle with the prosciutto pieces and season well. Serve immediately.

150 g (5 oz) spiral pasta
4 thick beef sausages
2 tablespoons olive oil
1 large red onion, cut into wedges
1 cup (250 g/8 oz) tomato pasta sauce
4 small ripe tomatoes, peeled, seeded and chopped
2 tablespoons chopped fresh flat-leaf parsley

1   Cook the pasta in a large pan of rapidly boiling salted water until al dente. Drain well and return to the pan to keep warm, reserving $^1/_4$ cup (60 ml/2 fl oz) of the cooking water.

2   Meanwhile, prick the sausages all over with a fork. Heat a non-stick frying pan and cook the sausages over medium heat, turning often, for 5 minutes, or until cooked. Cut into thick diagonal slices and set aside.

3   Clean the frying pan and heat the oil. Cook the onion wedges over medium heat for 3 minutes, or until soft. Add the tomato pasta sauce and the tomato. Cook for 5 minutes, or until the tomato has softened. Add the sliced sausage and heat through for 1 minute.

4   Toss the pasta through the sauce, adding a little of the reserved pasta water, if necessary. Sprinkle with parsley and serve.

INGREDIENTS

2 teaspoons olive oil
2 rashers bacon, chopped
2–3 cloves garlic, crushed
1 onion, finely chopped
2 spring onions, finely chopped
250 g (8 oz) ricotta
$1/2$ cup (30 g/1 oz) finely chopped fresh basil
325 g (11 oz) penne
8 cherry tomatoes, halved

1 Heat the oil in a pan, add the bacon, garlic, onion and spring onion and stir over medium heat for 5 minutes, or until cooked. Remove from the heat, stir in the ricotta and chopped basil and beat until smooth.

2 Cook the pasta in a large pan of rapidly boiling salted water until al dente. Just prior to draining the pasta, add about a cup of the pasta cooking water to the ricotta mixture to thin the sauce. Add more water if you prefer an even thinner sauce. Season with salt and pepper.

3 Drain the pasta and stir the sauce and tomato halves through the pasta. Garnish with tiny fresh basil leaves.

INGREDIENTS

500 g (1 lb) pasta shells or gnocchi
2 tablespoons olive oil
400 g (13 oz) thin Italian sausages
1 red onion, finely chopped
2 cloves garlic, finely chopped
2 x 415 g (13 oz) cans chopped tomatoes
1 teaspoon caster sugar
35 g (1 oz) fresh basil, torn
$1/2$ cup (45 g/$1^1/2$ oz) grated pecorino cheese

1   Cook the pasta in a large pan of rapidly boiling salted water until al dente. Drain and return to the pan to keep warm. Meanwhile, heat 2 teaspoons of the oil in a large frying pan. Add the sausages and cook, turning, for 5 minutes, or until well browned and cooked through. Drain on paper towels, then slice when cooled enough to hold. Keep warm.

2   Wipe clean the frying pan and heat the remaining oil. Add the onion and garlic and cook over medium heat for 2 minutes, or until the onion has softened. Add the tomato, sugar and 1 cup (250 ml/8 fl oz) water and season well. Reduce the heat and simmer for 12 minutes, or until thickened and reduced a little.

3   Pour the sauce over the pasta and stir through the sausage, basil and half the cheese. Serve hot, sprinkled with the remaining cheese.

INGREDIENTS

4 cloves garlic, unpeeled
⅓ cup (80 ml/2¾ fl oz) olive oil
250 g (8 oz) cherry tomatoes
300 g (10 oz) short cut bacon (see note)
350 g (11 oz) fresh fettucine
1 tablespoon white wine vinegar
2 tablespoons roughly chopped fresh basil
2 ripe avocados, diced
whole fresh basil leaves, to garnish

1 Preheat the oven to moderately hot 200°C (400°F/Gas 6). Place the garlic at one end of a roasting tin and drizzle with 2 tablespoons of the olive oil. Place the tomatoes at the other end and season well. Bake for 10 minutes, then remove the garlic. Return the tomatoes to the oven for a further 5–10 minutes, or until soft.

2 Cook the bacon under a hot grill for 4–5 minutes each side, or until crisp and golden. Roughly chop. Meanwhile, cook the pasta in a large saucepan of boiling water until al dente. Drain well and transfer to a large bowl. Drizzle 1 tablespoon of the olive oil over the pasta and toss well. Season to taste with salt and freshly ground black pepper and keep warm.

3 Slit the skin of each garlic clove and squeeze the garlic out. Place in a screw-top jar with the vinegar, chopped basil and remaining oil and shake well to combine. Add the tomatoes and their juices, bacon and avocado to the fettucine, pour on the dressing and toss well. Garnish with the basil leaves and serve with a green salad and crusty bread.

NOTE Short cut bacon is the meaty end of the bacon rasher and is also sold as eye bacon.

FETTUCINE WITH CHERRY TOMATOES, AVOCADO AND BACON

PENNE WITH PUMPKIN, BAKED RICOTTA AND PROSCIUTTO

500 g (1 lb) penne
460 g (15 oz) butternut pumpkin, cut into small cubes
1/4 cup (60 ml/2 fl oz) extra virgin olive oil
2 cloves garlic, crushed
100 g (3 1/2 oz) semi-dried tomatoes, chopped
4 slices prosciutto, chopped
250 g (8 oz) baked ricotta, cut into small cubes
3 tablespoons shredded fresh basil

1 Cook the pasta in a large pan of rapidly boiling salted water until al dente. Drain well. Meanwhile, cook the pumpkin in a saucepan of boiling water for 10–12 minutes, or until just tender, then drain.

2 Heat the oil in a large saucepan, add the garlic and cook over medium heat for 30 seconds. Add the tomato, prosciutto, pumpkin and penne and toss gently over low heat for 1–2 minutes, or until heated through.

3 Add the baked ricotta and the basil, season with salt and cracked black pepper and serve immediately.

400 g (13 oz) farfalle
2 tablespoons extra virgin olive oil
250 g (8 oz) bacon, chopped
1 red onion, finely chopped
250 g (8 oz) baby spinach leaves
1–2 tablespoons sweet chilli sauce
$1/4$ cup (30 g/1 oz) crumbled feta cheese

1 Cook the pasta in a large pan of rapidly boiling salted water until al dente. Drain and return to the pan to keep warm.

2 Meanwhile, heat the oil in a frying pan, add the bacon and cook over medium heat for 3 minutes, or until golden. Add the onion and cook for a further 4 minutes, or until softened. Toss the spinach leaves through the onion and bacon mixture for 30 seconds, or until just wilted.

3 Add the bacon and spinach mixture to the drained pasta, then stir in the sweet chilli sauce. Season to taste with salt and cracked black pepper and toss well. Spoon into warm pasta bowls and scatter with the crumbled feta. Serve immediately.

FARFALLE WITH SPINACH AND BACON

CREAMY PASTA GNOCCHI WITH PEAS AND PROSCIUTTO

100 g (3½ oz) thinly sliced prosciutto
3 teaspoons oil
2 eggs
1 cup (250 ml/8 fl oz) cream
⅓ cup (35 g/1¼ oz) finely grated Parmesan
2 tablespoons chopped fresh flat-leaf parsley
1 tablespoon chopped fresh chives
250 g (8 oz) fresh or frozen peas
500 g (1 lb) pasta gnocchi

1 Cut the prosciutto into 5 mm (¼ inch) wide strips. Heat the oil in a frying pan over medium heat, add the prosciutto and cook for 2 minutes, or until crisp. Drain on paper towels. Place the eggs, cream, Parmesan and herbs in a bowl and whisk well.

2 Bring a large saucepan of salted water to the boil. Add the peas and cook for 5 minutes, or until just tender. Leaving the pan on the heat, use a slotted spoon and transfer the peas to the bowl of cream mixture, and then add ¼ cup (60 ml/2 fl oz) of the cooking liquid to the same bowl. Using a potato masher or the back of a fork, roughly mash the peas.

3 Add the gnocchi to the boiling water and cook until al dente. Drain well, then return to the pan. Add the cream mixture, then warm through over low heat, gently stirring for about 30 seconds until the gnocchi is coated in the sauce. Season to taste with salt and cracked black pepper. Divide among warmed plates, top with the prosciutto and serve immediately.

NOTE Be careful not to overheat or cook for too long as the egg will begin to set and the result will look like a scrambled egg sauce.

INGREDIENTS

2 onions, sliced
2 bay leaves, crushed
1.5 kg (3 lb) veal shin, cut into osso buco pieces (see note)
1 cup (250 ml/8 fl oz) red wine
2 x 400 g (13 oz) cans crushed tomatoes
1$\frac{1}{2}$ cups (375 ml/12 fl oz) beef stock
2 teaspoons chopped fresh rosemary
400 g (13 oz) penne
1 cup (150 g/5 oz) frozen peas

1 Preheat the oven to hot 220°C (425°F/Gas 7). Scatter the onion over the bottom of a large roasting tin, lightly spray with oil and place the bay leaves and veal pieces on top. Season with salt and pepper. Roast for 10–15 minutes, or until the veal is browned. Take care that the onion doesn't burn.

2 Pour the wine over the veal and return to the oven for a further 5 minutes. Reduce the heat to moderate 180°C (350°F/Gas 4), remove the tin from the oven and pour on the tomato, stock and 1 teaspoon of the rosemary. Cover with foil and return to the oven. Cook for 2 hours, or until the veal is starting to fall from the bone. Remove the foil and cook for a further 15 minutes, or until the meat loosens away from the bone and the liquid has evaporated slightly.

3 Cook the pasta in a large pan of rapidly boiling salted water until al dente. Drain and return to the pan to keep warm. Meanwhile, remove the veal from the oven and cool slightly. Add the peas and remaining rosemary and place over a hotplate. Cook over medium heat for 5 minutes, or until the peas are cooked. Serve the pasta topped with the ragout.

NOTE Most butchers sell veal shin cut into osso buco pieces. If sold in a whole piece, ask the butcher to cut it for you (the pieces are about 3–4 cm thick). It is also available at some supermarkets. You can either remove the meat from the bone before serving, or leave it on.

PENNE WITH VEAL RAGOUT

INGREDIENTS

400 g (13 oz) pasta
1 tablespoon olive oil
180 g (6 oz) streaky bacon, thinly sliced (see note)
500 g (1 lb) Roma tomatoes, roughly chopped
$^1/_2$ cup (125 ml/4 fl oz) thick cream
2 tablespoons sun-dried tomato pesto
2 tablespoons finely chopped fresh flat-leaf parsley
$^1/_2$ cup (50 g/1$^3/_4$ oz) finely grated Parmesan

1   Cook the pasta in a large pan of rapidly boiling salted water until al dente. Drain and return
     to the pan to keep warm. Meanwhile, heat the oil in a frying pan, add the bacon and cook
     over high heat for 2 minutes, or until starting to brown. Reduce the heat to medium, add
     the tomato and cook, stirring frequently, for 2 minutes, or until the tomato has softened but
     still holds its shape.

2   Add the cream and tomato pesto and stir until heated through. Remove from the heat, add
     the parsley, then toss the sauce through the pasta with the grated Parmesan.

NOTE Streaky bacon is the tail fatty ends of bacon rashers and adds flavour to the dish. You can
      use ordinary bacon rashers if you prefer.

INGREDIENTS

450 g (14 oz) pork fillet
3–4 teaspoons cracked black peppercorns
90 g (3 oz) butter
250 g (8 oz) pasta
1 onion, halved and thinly sliced
2 large zucchini, thinly sliced
$2/_3$ cup (20 g/$3/_4$ oz) fresh basil, torn
$3/_4$ cup (150 g/5 oz) baby black olives
$1/_2$ cup (60 g/2 oz) grated Romano cheese

1　Cut the pork fillet in half widthways and roll in the cracked peppercorns and some salt. Heat half the butter in a large deep frying pan, add the pork and cook for 4 minutes each side, or until golden brown and just cooked through. Remove from the pan and cut into thin slices, then set aside and keep warm.

2　Cook the pasta in a large pan of rapidly boiling salted water until al dente. Drain and return to the pan to keep warm. Meanwhile, melt the remaining butter in the frying pan, add the onion and cook, stirring, over medium heat for about 3 minutes, or until soft. Add the zucchini and toss for 5 minutes, or until starting to soften. Add the basil, olives, sliced pork and any juices and toss well. Stir the pork mixture through the hot pasta, then season well. Serve immediately, topped with the cheese.

INGREDIENTS

500 g (1 lb) good-quality Italian sausages
2 tablespoons olive oil
3 cloves garlic, chopped
1 teaspoon fennel seeds
$^1/_2$ teaspoon chilli flakes
2 x 425 g (14 oz) cans crushed tomatoes
500 g (1 lb) bucatini
1 teaspoon balsamic vinegar
$^1/_4$ cup (7 g/$^1/_4$ oz) loosely packed fresh basil, chopped

1   Heat a frying pan over high heat, add the sausages and cook, turning, for 8–10 minutes, or until well browned and cooked through. Remove, cool slightly and slice thinly on the diagonal.

2   Heat the oil in a saucepan, add the garlic and cook over medium heat for 1 minute. Add the fennel seeds and chilli flakes and cook for a further minute. Stir in the tomato and bring to the boil, then reduce the heat and simmer, covered, for 20 minutes. Meanwhile, cook the pasta in a large pan of rapidly boiling salted water until al dente. Drain and return to the pan to keep warm.

3   Add the sausages to the sauce and cook, uncovered, for 5 minutes to heat through. Stir in the balsamic vinegar and basil. Divide the pasta among four bowls, top with the sauce and serve.

500 g (1 lb) fresh linguine
1 tablespoon butter
2 large cloves garlic, chopped
150 g (5 oz) marinated artichokes, drained and quartered
150 g (5 oz) sliced leg ham, cut into strips
300 ml (10 fl oz) cream
2 teaspoons roughly grated lemon rind
$^1/_2$ cup (15 g/$^1/_2$ oz) fresh basil, torn
$^1/_3$ cup (35 g/1 oz) grated Parmesan

1 Cook the pasta in a large pan of rapidly boiling salted water until al dente. Drain and return to the pan to keep warm. Meanwhile, melt the butter in a large frying pan, add the garlic and cook over medium heat for 1 minute, or until fragrant. Add the artichokes and ham and cook for a further 2 minutes.

2 Add the cream and lemon rind, reduce the heat and simmer for 5 minutes, gently breaking up the artichokes with a wooden spoon. Pour the sauce over the pasta, then add the basil and Parmesan and toss well until the pasta is evenly coated. Serve immediately.

LINGUINE WITH HAM, ARTICHOKE AND LEMON SAUCE

PAPPARDELLE WITH SALAMI, LEEK AND PROVOLONE CHEESE

375 g (12 oz) pappardelle

2 tablespoons olive oil

2 leeks, thinly sliced (including some of the green section)

2 tablespoons white wine

2 x 400 g (13 oz) cans diced tomatoes

150 g (5 oz) sliced mild salami, cut into strips

$1/4$ cup (7 g/$1/4$ oz) fresh basil leaves, torn

125 g (4 oz) provolone cheese, sliced into strips

30 g (1 oz) grated Parmesan

1 Cook the pasta in a large pan of rapidly boiling salted water until al dente. Drain and return to the pan to keep warm. Meanwhile, heat the olive oil in a large deep frying pan, add the leek and cook over low heat for 4 minutes, or until soft but not browned. Increase the heat to medium, add the wine and stir until almost evaporated.

2 Add the tomato and salami, season with salt and cracked black pepper and simmer for 5 minutes, or until reduced slightly. Toss the tomato sauce mixture, basil and provolone lightly through the pasta. Sprinkle with Parmesan and serve.

INGREDIENTS

500 g (1 lb) fresh tomato fettucine
600 g (1¼ lb) chicken tenderloins
40 g (1¼ oz) butter
3 eggs
300 ml (10 fl oz) cream
½ cup (50 g/1½ oz) grated Parmesan
shaved Parmesan and fresh basil leaves, to garnish

1 Cook the pasta in a large pan of rapidly boiling salted water until al dente. Drain and return to the pan to keep warm.

2 Trim and slice the tenderloins in half on the diagonal. Melt the butter in a frying pan and cook the chicken for 4–5 minutes, or until browned. Lightly beat the eggs and cream together and stir in the grated Parmesan. Season with salt to taste and stir through the chicken.

3 Combine the chicken and cream mixture with the fettucine in the frying pan. Reduce the heat and cook, stirring constantly, for 10–15 seconds, or until the sauce is slightly thickened. Do not keep on the heat too long or the eggs will set and scramble. Season with black pepper and serve, garnished with the extra Parmesan and basil leaves.

INGREDIENTS

650 g (1 lb 5 oz) pumpkin
2 tablespoons olive oil
500 g (1 lb) ricotta cheese
⅓ cup (50 g/1¾ oz) pine nuts, toasted
¾ cup (35 g/1 oz) fresh basil
2 cloves garlic, crushed
35 g (1 oz) Parmesan, grated
125 g (4 oz) fresh lasagne sheets
185 g (6 oz) mozzarella, grated

1 Preheat the oven to moderate 180°C (350°F/Gas 4). Lightly grease a baking tray. Cut the pumpkin into thin slices and arrange in a single layer on the tray. Brush with oil and cook for 1 hour, or until softened, turning halfway through cooking.

2 Place the ricotta, pine nuts, basil, garlic and Parmesan in a bowl and mix well with a wooden spoon.

3 Brush a square 20 cm (8 inch) ovenproof dish with oil. Cook the pasta according to the packet instructions. Arrange one third of the pasta sheets over the base of the dish and spread with the ricotta mixture. Top with half of the remaining lasagne sheets.

4 Arrange the pumpkin evenly over the pasta with as few gaps as possible. Season with salt and cracked black pepper and top with the final layer of pasta sheets. Sprinkle with mozzarella. Bake for 20–25 minutes, or until the cheese is golden. Leave for 10 minutes, then cut into squares.

NOTE If the pasta has no cooking instructions, blanch them one at a time until softened. Then drain and spread on tea towels to dry.

250 g (8 oz) baby bok choy, leaves separated

600 g (1$^1/_4$ lb) fresh pappardelle

1 Chinese roast duck, skin removed (see note)

$^1/_3$ cup (80 ml/3$^3/_4$ fl oz) peanut oil

3 cloves garlic, crushed

3 teaspoons grated fresh ginger

$^3/_4$ cup (35 g/1 oz) chopped fresh coriander leaves

2 tablespoons hoisin sauce

2 tablespoons oyster sauce

1   Bring a large pan of water to the boil and blanch the bok choy for 1–2 minutes, or until tender but still crisp. Remove with a slotted spoon and keep warm. Cook the pasta in the water until al dente. Drain well and return to the pan to keep warm.

2   Remove and shred the duck meat. Heat the peanut oil in a small pan over high heat until smoking. Remove from the heat and cool for 1 minute, then swirl in the garlic and ginger to infuse the oil. Be careful not to allow the garlic to burn or it will turn bitter.

3   Pour the hot oil over the pasta and add the bok choy, duck, coriander, hoisin and oyster sauces. Toss well, season and serve immediately.

NOTE   Chinese roast duck can be bought from Asian barbecue food shops or restaurants.

SMOKED SALMON PASTA

500 g (1 lb) pasta
1 tablespoon olive oil
4 spring onions, finely chopped
180 g (6 oz) button mushrooms, sliced
1 cup (250 ml/8 fl oz) dry white wine
300 ml (10 fl oz) cream
1 tablespoon finely chopped fresh dill
1 tablespoon lemon juice
90 g (3 oz) Parmesan, grated
200 g (6$^1/_2$ oz) smoked salmon, cut into strips
shaved Parmesan and lemon wedges, to serve

1 Cook the pasta in a large pan of rapidly boiling salted water until al dente. Drain and return to the pan to keep warm.

2 Meanwhile, heat the oil in a small saucepan, add the spring onion and mushrooms and cook over medium heat for 1−2 minutes, or until soft. Add the wine and cream and bring to the boil, then reduce the heat and simmer for 1 minute.

3 Pour the mushroom sauce over the pasta and stir through the dill and lemon juice. Add the Parmesan and stir until warmed through. Remove from the heat and stir in the smoked salmon. Season with pepper and serve with Parmesan shavings and lemon wedges.

20 large scallops with roe
250 g (8 oz) angel hair pasta
150 ml (5 fl oz) extra virgin olive oil
2 cloves garlic, finely chopped
$^1/_4$ cup (60 ml/2 fl oz) white wine
1 tablespoon lemon juice
100 g (3$^1/_2$ oz) baby rocket leaves
$^1/_2$ cup (30 g/1 oz) chopped fresh coriander leaves

1 Pull or trim any veins, membrane or hard white muscle from the scallops. Pat the scallops dry with paper towels. Cook the pasta in a large pan of rapidly boiling salted water until al dente. Drain and transfer to a bowl. Toss with 1 tablespoon of the oil.

2 Meanwhile, heat 1 tablespoon oil in a frying pan, add the garlic and cook for a few seconds, or until fragrant. Do not brown. Add the wine and lemon juice, and remove from the heat.

3 Heat a chargrill pan or barbecue grill plate over high heat and brush with a little oil. Season the scallops with salt and pepper and cook for 1 minute each side, or until just cooked. Gently reheat the garlic mixture, add the rocket and stir over medium heat for 1–2 minutes, or until wilted. Toss through the pasta and mix together well. Add the remaining oil and half the coriander and mix well. Divide the pasta among four bowls, arrange the scallops over the top and garnish with the remaining coriander.

ANGEL HAIR PASTA WITH GARLIC, SCALLOPS AND ROCKET

INGREDIENTS

500 g (1 lb) pappardelle pasta

50 g (1³/₄ oz) butter

4 cloves garlic, crushed

150 g (5 oz) oyster mushrooms

800 g (1 lb 10 oz) raw prawns, peeled and deveined

2 x 400 g (13 oz) salmon fillets, skin removed, cut into small cubes

1 cup (250 ml/8 fl oz) white wine

1 cup (250 ml/8 fl oz) fish stock

¹/₄ teaspoon saffron threads

400 ml (13 fl oz) crème fraîche

125 g (4 oz) sugar snap peas or snow peas

1   Cook the pasta in a large pan of rapidly boiling salted water until al dente. Drain and return to the pan to keep warm.

2   Meanwhile, melt the butter in a large deep frying pan, add the garlic and oyster mushrooms and cook for 1 minute. Add the prawns and salmon and cook for 2–3 minutes, or until the prawns are cooked and the salmon starts to flake but is still rare in the centre. Be careful not to burn the garlic. Transfer to a bowl.

3   Pour the wine and stock into the pan and add the saffron. Scrape the bottom of the pan with a wooden spoon. Bring to the boil, then reduce the heat and simmer rapidly for 5 minutes, or until reduced by half. Add the crème fraîche and sugar snap peas and stir through. Bring to the boil, then reduce the heat and simmer, stirring occasionally, for 3–4 minutes, until the liquid has slightly thickened.

4   Return the seafood and any juices to the pan and gently stir over medium heat until warmed through. Serve immediately over the pasta.

INGREDIENTS

375 g (12 oz) spaghetti
1/3 cup (80 ml/2 3/4 fl oz) olive oil
2 onions, finely chopped
3 cloves garlic, finely chopped
1/2 teaspoon chilli flakes
6 large ripe tomatoes, diced
4 tablespoons capers in brine, rinsed, drained
7–8 anchovies in oil, drained, minced
150 g (5 oz) Kalamata olives
3 tablespoons chopped fresh flat-leaf parsley

1 Cook the pasta in a large pan of rapidly boiling salted water until al dente. Drain and return to the pan to keep warm.

2 Meanwhile, heat the oil in a saucepan, add the onion and cook over medium heat for 5 minutes. Add the garlic and chilli flakes, and cook for 30 seconds, then add the tomato, capers and anchovies. Simmer over low heat for 5–10 minutes, or until thick and pulpy, then stir in the olives and parsley.

3 Stir the pasta through the sauce. Season and serve immediately with crusty bread.

INGREDIENTS

2 tablespoons salt
2 tablespoons plain flour
1 kg (2 lb) clams or pipis
500 g (1 lb) shell pasta
1 tablespoon olive oil
2 cloves garlic, crushed
2 x 425 g (14 oz) cans crushed tomatoes
$^1/_4$ cup (60 ml/2 fl oz) red wine
2 tablespoons chopped fresh parsley
1 teaspoon sugar

1   Blend the salt and plain flour with enough water to make a paste. Add to a large pan of cold water and soak the shellfish overnight. This will draw out sand from inside the shells. Scrub the shells well. Rinse and drain.

2   Cook the pasta in a large pan of rapidly boiling salted water until al dente. Drain and return to the pan to keep warm. Meanwhile, heat the oil in a large pan. Add the garlic and cook over low heat for 30 seconds. Add the tomatoes, wine, parsley and sugar and season. Stir and bring to the boil. Reduce the heat and simmer, stirring occasionally, for 5 minutes.

3   Add the clams to the sauce and cook for 3–5 minutes, stirring occasionally, until opened. Discard any clams that do not open in the cooking time. Serve over the pasta.

INGREDIENTS

^{1}/$_2$ cup (125 ml/4 fl oz) dry white wine

pinch of saffron threads

500 g (1 lb) fresh saffron or plain angel-hair pasta

1 tablespoon virgin olive oil

30 g (1 oz) butter

750 g (1^1/$_2$ lb) raw prawns, peeled and deveined

3 cloves garlic, crushed

100 g (3^1/$_2$ oz) butter, for pan-frying, extra

^{1}/$_2$ preserved lemon, rinsed, pith and flesh removed, cut into thin strips

1 tablespoon lemon juice

4 spring onions, thinly sliced

4 kaffir lime leaves, thinly shredded

^{1}/$_2$ cup (125 ml/4 fl oz) chicken stock

2 tablespoons snipped chives

1   Place the wine and saffron in a small saucepan and boil for 3 minutes, or until reduced by half. Remove from the heat.

2   Cook the pasta in a large pan of rapidly boiling salted water until al dente. Drain and return to the pan to keep warm.

3   Heat the oil and butter in a large frying pan and cook the prawns in batches over high heat for 3 minutes, or until pink and tender. Cut into thirds, then transfer to a plate and keep warm.

4   Add the garlic and extra butter to the same pan and cook over medium heat for 3 minutes, or until golden. Add the wine and stir to remove any sediment from the bottom of the pan. Add the preserved lemon, lemon juice, spring onion, lime leaves and stock and bring to the boil, then reduce the heat and simmer for 2 minutes.

5   Return the prawns to the frying pan and heat through. Serve the pasta topped with some of the prawns and sauce and sprinkle with chives.

CAJUN SCALLOPS WITH PASTA AND BUTTERY CORN SAUCE

350 g (11 oz) small pasta shells
20 large scallops, without roe
2 tablespoons Cajun spice mix
2 tablespoons corn oil
250 g (8 oz) butter
3 cloves garlic, crushed
400 g (13 oz) can corn kernels, drained
¼ cup (60 ml/2 fl oz) lime juice
4 tablespoons finely chopped fresh coriander leaves

1   Cook the pasta in a large pan of rapidly boiling salted water until al dente. Drain and return to the pan to keep warm. Meanwhile, pat the scallops dry with paper towel and lightly coat in the spice mix. Heat the oil in a large frying pan and cook the scallops for 1 minute each side over high heat (ensuring they are well spaced), then remove from the pan, cover and keep warm.

2   Reduce the heat to medium, add the butter and cook for 4 minutes, or until foaming and golden brown. Remove from the heat, add the garlic, corn and lime juice. Gently toss the corn mixture through the pasta with 2 tablespoons of the coriander and season well. Divide among four serving plates, top with the scallops, drizzle with any juices and sprinkle with the remaining coriander.

Scallops should not be crowded when they are cooked or they will release all their juices, causing them to stew and toughen.

600 g (1¹/₄ lb) broccoli, cut into florets
500 g (1 lb) orecchiette
1 tablespoon olive oil
4 cloves garlic, finely chopped
8 anchovy fillets, roughly chopped
1 cup (250 ml/8 fl oz) cream
1 cup (30 g/1 oz) fresh basil, torn
2 teaspoons finely grated lemon rind
100 g (3¹/₂ oz) Parmesan, grated

1 Blanch the broccoli in a large saucepan of boiling salted water for 3–4 minutes. Remove and plunge into chilled water. Drain well with a slotted spoon. Cook the pasta in a large pan of rapidly boiling salted water until al dente. Drain and return to the pan to keep warm, reserving 2 tablespoons of the cooking water.

2 Meanwhile, heat the oil in a frying pan over medium heat. Add the garlic and anchovies and cook for 1–2 minutes, or until the garlic begins to turn golden. Add the broccoli and cook for a further 5 minutes. Add the cream and half the basil and cook for 10 minutes, or until the cream has reduced and slightly thickened and the broccoli is very tender.

3 Purée half the mixture in a food processor until nearly smooth, then return to the pan with the lemon rind, half the Parmesan and 2 tablespoons of the reserved water. Stir together well, then season. Add the warm pasta and remaining basil, and toss until well combined. Sprinkle with the remaining Parmesan and serve immediately.

PASTA WITH ANCHOVIES, BROCCOLI AND BASIL

INGREDIENTS

4 x 200 g (6$^1/_2$ oz) tuna steaks
$^2/_3$ cup (170 ml/5$^1/_2$ oz) balsamic vinegar
$^1/_2$ cup (125 ml/4 fl oz) good-quality olive oil
1 lemon
1 clove garlic, finely chopped
1 red onion, finely chopped
2 tablespoons capers, rinsed and dried
$^1/_2$ cup (15 g/$^1/_2$ oz) fresh flat-leaf parsley, finely chopped
500 g (1 lb) fresh fettucine

1   Place the tuna steaks in a non-metallic dish and cover with the balsamic vinegar. Turn to coat evenly and marinate for 10 minutes. Heat 2 tablespoons of the oil in a large frying pan over medium heat and cook the tuna for 2–3 minutes each side. Remove from the pan, cut into small cubes and transfer to a bowl.

2   Finely grate the rind from the lemon to give $^1/_2$ teaspoon rind, then squeeze the lemon to give $^1/_4$ cup (60 ml/2 fl oz) juice. Wipe the frying pan clean, and heat 2 tablespoons of the olive oil over medium heat, then add the garlic and cook for 30 seconds. Stir in the chopped onion and cook for 2 minutes. Add the lemon rind and capers and cook for 1 minute, then stir in the parsley and cook for 1 minute. Add the lemon juice and remaining oil and gently toss together. Season to taste.

3   Cook the pasta in a large pan of rapidly boiling salted water until al dente. Drain, return to the pan and toss with the caper mixture. Divide the pasta among serving bowls and arrange the tuna pieces over the top.

INGREDIENTS

800 g (1 lb 10 oz) vine-ripened tomatoes
375 g (12 oz) spaghetti
3 x 125 g (4 oz) cans smoked tuna slices in oil
1 red onion, chopped
2 cloves garlic, crushed
1 teaspoon sugar
150 g (5 oz) black olives
2 tablespoons chopped fresh basil
75 g (2^1/$_2$ oz) feta cheese, crumbled

1   Score a cross in the base of each tomato. Place the tomatoes in a bowl of boiling water for 1 minute, then plunge into cold water and peel the skin away from the cross. Cut in half and remove the seeds with a teaspoon. Roughly chop the flesh. Cook the pasta in a large pan of rapidly boiling salted water until al dente. Drain and return to the pan to keep warm.

2   Drain the oil from the tuna slices, reserving 1 tablespoon. Heat the reserved oil in a large saucepan, add the onion and cook over low heat for 3–4 minutes, or until soft but not brown. Add the garlic and cook for another minute, then add the chopped tomatoes and sugar. Cook over medium heat for 8–10 minutes, or until pulpy.

3   Add the tuna slices, olives and chopped basil, stir well and cook for 2 minutes, or until warmed through. Toss through the spaghetti and season with salt and cracked black pepper. Sprinkle with crumbled feta and serve.

INGREDIENTS

2 tablespoons olive oil
16 raw prawns, peeled and deveined
1 leek, chopped
6 cloves garlic, crushed
$1/2$ teaspoon dried chilli flakes
$1/2$ cup (125 ml/4 fl oz) dry white wine
200 ml ($6^1/2$ fl oz) cream
250 g (8 oz) angel hair pasta
3 tablespoons chopped fresh flat-leaf parsley

1   Heat half the oil in a frying pan, season the prawns with salt and pepper, add to the pan and cook over high heat for 2–3 minutes, or until cooked through. Remove from the pan, cover and keep warm.

2   Heat the remaining oil in the same pan, add the leek and cook, stirring, over medium heat for 2–3 minutes, or until softened. Add the garlic and chilli flakes and stir for 1 minute. Pour in the wine, reduce the heat and simmer for 4 minutes, or until reduced. Add the cream and simmer for 3 minutes, or until just thickened.

3   Meanwhile, cook the pasta in a large pan of rapidly boiling salted water until al dente. Drain and return to the pan to keep warm. Stir the parsley into the sauce and season well. Add to the pasta and stir to coat. Divide the pasta among bowls and top with the prawns.

INGREDIENTS

500 g (1 lb) mussels
1 kg (2 lb) clams
400 g (13 oz) spaghetti
2 tablespoons olive oil
4 French shallots, finely chopped
2 cloves garlic, crushed
1 cup (250 ml/8 fl oz) dry white wine
3 tablespoons chopped fresh flat-leaf parsley

1   Scrub the mussels with a stiff brush and remove any barnacles with a knife. Pull away the
beards. Discard any mussels or clams that are broken or open ones that do not close
when tapped on the work surface. Wash them both thoroughly under cold running water.
Cook the pasta in a large pan of rapidly boiling salted water until al dente. Drain and return
to the pan to keep warm.

2   Meanwhile, heat the oil in a large saucepan over medium heat and cook the shallots for
4 minutes, or until softened. Add the garlic and cook for a further 1 minute. Pour in the
wine, bring to the boil and cook for 2 minutes, or until reduced slightly. Add the clams and
mussels, tossing to coat them in the liquid, then cover the pan. Cook, shaking the pan
regularly, for about 3 minutes, or until the shells have opened. Discard any clams or
mussels that do not open in the cooking time. Toss the clam mixture through the
spaghetti, scatter with parsley and transfer to a warmed serving dish. Season and serve
with salad and bread.

SMOKED SALMON PASTA IN CHAMPAGNE SAUCE

375 g (12 oz) pappardelle
1 tablespoon olive oil
2 large cloves garlic, crushed
$1/2$ cup (125 ml/4 fl oz) Champagne
1 cup (250 ml/8 fl oz) thick cream
200 g (6$1/2$ oz) smoked salmon, cut into thin strips
2 tablespoons small capers in brine, rinsed and dried
2 tablespoons chopped fresh chives
2 tablespoons chopped fresh dill

1 Cook the pasta in a large pan of rapidly boiling salted water until al dente. Drain and keep warm. Heat the oil in a frying pan; cook the garlic over medium heat for 30 seconds. Pour in the Champagne and cook for 2–3 minutes, or until reduced slightly. Add the cream and cook for 3–4 minutes, or until thickened.

2 Toss the sauce and remaining ingredients with the pasta and serve.

INGREDIENTS

400 g (13 oz) pappardelle
60 g (2 oz) butter
4 large cloves garlic, crushed
250 g (8 oz) Swiss brown mushrooms, sliced
500 g (1 lb) fresh or frozen lobster tail meat or raw bug tails
$1/2$ cup (125 ml/4 fl oz) white wine
$1/2$ teaspoon saffron threads
700 ml (23 fl oz) thick cream
2 egg yolks

1   Cook the pasta in a large pan of rapidly boiling salted water until al dente. Drain and return to the pan to keep warm. Meanwhile, melt the butter in a large deep frying pan, add the garlic and mushrooms and cook over medium heat for 2–3 minutes, or until soft. Add the lobster and cook for 4–5 minutes, or until just cooked through. Remove from the pan.

2   Add the wine and saffron to the pan, scraping the bottom to collect any bits. Bring to the boil and cook for 2–3 minutes, or until reduced. Add the cream, reduce the heat and simmer for 5 minutes. Whisk through the egg yolks until thickened. Return the lobster mixture to the pan and stir until warmed through. Drain the pasta and divide among serving dishes. Spoon on the lobster sauce and season to taste. Serve immediately.

250 g (8 oz) fresh lasagne sheets
1 tablespoon olive oil
30 g (1 oz) butter
1 onion, finely chopped
2 cloves garlic, crushed
400 g (13 oz) raw medium prawns, peeled and deveined
500 g (1 lb) skinless firm white fish fillets, cut into 2 cm (¾ inch) pieces
250 g (8 oz) scallops with roe, membrane removed
750 g (1½ lb) bottled tomato pasta sauce
1 tablespoon tomato paste
1 teaspoon soft brown sugar
½ cup (60 g/2 oz) grated Cheddar
¼ cup (25 g/¾ oz) grated Parmesan

Cheese Sauce

120 g (4 oz) butter
⅔ cup (85 g/3 oz) plain flour
1.5 litres milk
2 cups (250 g/8 oz) grated Cheddar
1 cup (100 g/3½ oz) grated Parmesan

1 Preheat the oven to moderate 180°C (350°F/Gas 4). Lightly grease a 27 cm x 21 cm (10¾ inch x 8½ inch), 2.5 litre ovenproof dish and line with the lasagne sheets.

2 Heat the oil and butter in a large saucepan. Add the onion and cook for 2–3 minutes, or until softened. Add the garlic and cook for 30 seconds. Cook the prawns and fish pieces for 2 minutes, then add the scallops and cook for 1 minute. Stir in the pasta sauce, tomato paste and sugar and simmer for 5 minutes.

3 For the cheese sauce, melt the butter over low heat in a saucepan, stir in the flour and cook for 1 minute, or until pale and foaming. Remove from the heat and gradually stir in the milk. Return to the heat and stir until the sauce boils and thickens. Reduce the heat, simmer for 2 minutes, then stir in the cheeses. Season, to taste.

4 Spoon one-third of the seafood sauce over the lasagne sheets. Top with one-third of the cheese sauce. Arrange lasagne sheets over the top. Repeat to make three layers. Sprinkle with the combined cheeses and bake for 30 minutes or until golden. Leave for 10 minutes before slicing.

INGREDIENTS

1.5 kg (3 lb) orange sweet potato, cut into small cubes
$^1/_3$ cup (80 ml/2$^3/_4$ fl oz) olive oil
4 cloves garlic, crushed
2 tablespoons butter
4 red onions, sliced into thin wedges
500 g (1 lb) fresh basil fettucine
400 g (13 oz) soft feta cheese, diced
200 g (6$^1/_2$ oz) small black olives
$^1/_2$ cup (30 g/1 oz) firmly packed fresh basil, torn

1   Preheat the oven to moderately hot 200°C (400°F/Gas 6). Place the sweet potato, oil and garlic in a bowl and toss to coat the sweet potato. Lay out the sweet potato in a roasting tin and roast for 15 minutes. Turn and roast for another 15 minutes, until tender and golden—make sure the sweet potato is not too soft or it will not hold its shape. Keep warm.

2   Meanwhile, melt the butter in a deep frying pan and cook the onion over low heat, stirring occasionally, for 25–30 minutes, or until soft and slightly caramelised.

3   Cook the pasta in a large pan of rapidly boiling salted water until al dente. Drain and return to the pan. Add the onion to the pasta and toss together. Add the sweet potato, feta, olives and basil and gently toss. Serve drizzled with extra virgin olive oil.

INGREDIENTS

400 g (13 oz) cavatelli
90 g (3 oz) butter
2 cloves garlic, crushed
3 tablespoons chopped fresh chives
3 tablespoons shredded fresh basil
1 tablespoon shredded fresh sage
1 teaspoon fresh thyme
$^1/_4$ cup (60 ml/2 fl oz) warm vegetable stock
60 g (2 oz) Pecorino cheese, grated

1   Cook the pasta in a large pan of rapidly boiling salted water until al dente. Drain and return to the pan to keep warm. Meanwhile, heat the butter in a small saucepan over medium heat, add the garlic and cook for 1 minute, or until fragrant. Add the chives, basil, sage and thyme and cook for a further minute.

2   Add the herb mixture and stock to the pasta in the pan. Return to the heat for 2–3 minutes, or until warmed through. Season to taste, add the Pecorino and stir well. Divide among bowls and garnish with sage leaves.

NOTE   Pecorino is Italian sheep's milk cheese with a sharp flavour. If you can't find it, use Parmesan instead.

INGREDIENTS

1 litre vegetable or chicken stock
350 g (11 oz) penne
$^1/_3$ cup (80 ml/2$^3/_4$ fl oz) virgin olive oil, plus extra for serving
1 onion, chopped
2 carrots, diced
3 celery stalks, diced
3 cloves garlic, crushed
1 tablespoon plus 1 teaspoon chopped fresh thyme
400 g (13 oz) can lentils, drained

1 Boil the chicken stock in a large saucepan for 10 minutes, or until reduced by half. Meanwhile, cook the pasta in a large pan of rapidly boiling salted water until al dente. Drain well and toss with 2 tablespoons of the olive oil.

2 Heat the remaining oil in a large, deep frying pan, add the onion, carrot and celery and cook over medium heat for 10 minutes, or until browned. Add two-thirds of the crushed garlic and 1 tablespoon of the thyme and cook for a further 1 minute. Add the stock, bring to the boil and cook for 8 minutes, or until tender. Stir in the lentils and heat through.

3 Stir in the remaining garlic and thyme and season well—the stock should be slightly syrupy at this point. Combine the pasta with the lentil sauce in a large bowl and drizzle with virgin olive oil to serve.

INGREDIENTS

1 tablespoon olive oil

2 cloves garlic, crushed

1 onion, chopped

1 carrot, grated

1 celery stalk, diced

125 g (4 oz) mushrooms, chopped

600 g (1¼ lb) minced beef

2½ cups (600 ml/20 fl oz) Italian tomato passata

1 teaspoon dried oregano leaves

300 g (10 oz) instant lasagne sheets

1 cup (100 g/3½ oz) grated Parmesan

Cheese Sauce

60 g (2 oz) butter

⅓ cup (40 g/1¼ oz) plain flour

1 litre milk

½ teaspoon ground nutmeg

1 cup (125 g/4 oz) grated Cheddar

1   Heat the oil in a large heavy-based pan. Add the garlic, onion, carrot, celery and mushroom. Cook, stirring, over medium heat for 2–3 minutes, or until the onion has softened. Increase the heat, add the mince and stir for a further 3–4 minutes, or until the mince has browned and is well broken up.

2   Add the tomato passata, oregano and 2 cups (500 ml/16 fl oz) water. Bring to the boil, stirring, then lower the heat and simmer for 1 hour, or until the mixture has thickened. Stir occasionally.

3   To make the cheese sauce, melt the butter in a heavy-based pan. Add the flour and cook, stirring, for 1 minute until pale and foaming. Remove from the heat, gradually add the milk and stir until smooth. Return to the heat and stir continuously for 3–4 minutes, or until the sauce boils and thickens. Cook over low heat for 1 minute. Stir in the nutmeg and Cheddar. Season.

4   To assemble, preheat the oven to moderate 180°C (350°F/Gas 4). Grease a 2.5 litre baking dish. Arrange four lasagne sheets over the base of the baking dish. Spread one-third of the meat mixture over the sheets, then pour over about ¾ cup (185 ml/6 fl oz) of the cheese sauce. Repeat with two more layers of each. Top with the four remaining lasagne sheets, then with the remaining sauce and finish with the Parmesan. Bake for 45 minutes, or until golden. Leave to stand for 5 minutes before serving.

INGREDIENTS

¼ cup (60 ml/2 fl oz) olive oil

1 onion, finely chopped

2 cloves garlic, crushed

80 g (2¾ oz) pancetta, finely chopped

500 g (1 lb) beef mince

1 teaspoon chopped fresh oregano

60 g (2 oz) small button mushrooms, sliced

115 g (4 oz) chicken livers, trimmed and finely chopped

¼ teaspoon ground nutmeg

pinch cayenne pepper

¼ cup (60 ml/2 fl oz) dry white wine

2 tablespoons tomato paste

1½ cups (375 ml/12 fl oz) beef stock

2 tablespoons grated Parmesan

1 egg, beaten

150 g (5 oz) macaroni

100 g (3½ oz) ricotta cheese

2 tablespoons milk

pinch cayenne pepper, extra

pinch ground nutmeg, extra

1 egg, beaten, extra

1 cup (100 g/3½ oz) grated Parmesan, extra

Bechamel sauce

40 g (1¼ oz) butter

1½ tablespoons plain flour

pinch ground nutmeg

300 ml (10 fl oz) milk

1 small bay leaf

1 Preheat the oven to moderate 180°C (350°F/Gas 4). Lightly grease a 1.5 litre ovenproof dish. Heat the oil in a large frying pan over medium heat and cook the onion, garlic and pancetta, stirring, for 5 minutes, or until the onion is golden. Add the beef, increase the heat and stir for 5 minutes, or until browned.

2 Add the oregano, mushrooms, chicken livers, nutmeg and cayenne, season and cook for 2 minutes, or until the livers change colour. Add the wine and cook over high heat for 1 minute, or until evaporated. Stir in tomato paste and stock. Reduce heat and simmer for 45 minutes, or until thickened. Beat the Parmesan and egg together, and quickly stir into sauce.

3 Cook the macaroni in lightly salted boiling water until al dente. Blend the ricotta, milk, extra cayenne, extra nutmeg, extra egg and ¼ cup (25 g/¾ oz) extra Parmesan. Season. Drain the macaroni, add to the ricotta mixture and mix well.

4 To make the Béchamel sauce, melt the butter in a small saucepan. Stir in the flour and cook over low heat until beginning to turn golden, then stir in the nutmeg. Remove from the heat and gradually stir in the milk. Add the bay leaf and season. Return to low heat and simmer, stirring, until thickened. Discard the bay leaf.

5 Spread half the meat sauce in the dish, layer half the pasta over the top and sprinkle with half the remaining Parmesan. Layer with remaining meat sauce and pasta. Press down firmly with the back of a spoon. Spread the Béchamel sauce over the top and sprinkle with remaining Parmesan. Bake for 45–50 minutes, or until golden. Rest for 15 minutes before serving.

INGREDIENTS

24 conchiglione (large pasta shells)
200 g (6$\frac{1}{2}$ oz) prosciutto, roughly chopped
2 tablespoons chopped chives
1 cup (60 g/2 oz) chopped fresh basil
90 g (3 oz) butter
500 g (1 lb) ricotta
1 cup (150 g/5 oz) chopped sun-dried capsicum
1 cup (100 g/3$\frac{1}{2}$ oz) grated Parmesan
3 cups (750 g/1$\frac{1}{2}$ lb) bottled tomato pasta sauce

1   Preheat the oven to moderate 180°C (350°F/Gas 4). Cook the pasta in a large pan of rapidly boiling salted water until al dente. Drain well and return to the pan to keep warm. Place the prosciutto, chives and basil in a food processor or blender and pulse until chopped.

2   Melt the butter in a large frying pan over medium heat. Add the prosciutto mixture and cook for about 5 minutes, or until the prosciutto is golden and crisp. Transfer the mixture to a bowl, add the ricotta, capsicum and a quarter of the Parmesan. Stir well and season to taste.

3   Pour the pasta sauce into a 3-litre ovenproof dish. Spoon the ricotta mixture into the pasta shells and place in the dish. Sprinkle the remaining Parmesan over the shells and bake for 25–30 minutes, or until golden. Spoon the sauce over the shells and serve.

INGREDIENTS

85 g (3 oz) butter
1 onion, chopped
500 g (1 lb 2 oz) minced (ground) beef
800 g (1 lb 12 oz) bottled tomato pasta sauce
2 tablespoons tomato paste (purée)
250 g (9 oz) vermicelli or spaghettini
30 g (¹/₄ cup) plain (all-purpose) flour
375 ml (1¹/₄ cups) milk
155 g (1¹/₄ cups) grated Cheddar cheese

1 Preheat the oven to 180°C (350°F/Gas 4). Grease a 24 cm (9 inch) round deep springform tin. Melt 20 g (³/₄ oz) of the butter in a large deep frying pan and cook the onion over medium heat for 2–3 minutes, or until soft. Add the mince, breaking up any lumps with the back of a spoon, and cook for 4–5 minutes, or until browned. Stir in the pasta sauce and tomato paste, reduce the heat and simmer for 20–25 minutes. Season.

2 Cook the pasta in a large saucepan of boiling salted water until al dente. Drain and rinse. Meanwhile, melt the remaining butter in a saucepan over low heat. Stir in the flour and cook for 1 minute, or until pale and foaming. Remove from the heat and gradually stir in the milk. Return to the heat and stir constantly until the sauce boils and thickens. Reduce the heat and simmer for 2 minutes.

3 Spread half the pasta over the base of the tin, then cover with half the meat sauce. Cover with the remaining pasta, pressing it down. Spoon on the remaining meat sauce and then pour on the white sauce. Sprinkle with cheese and cook for 15 minutes. Stand for 10 minutes before removing from the tin. Cut into wedges.

200 g (7 oz) short curly pasta such as cotelli or fusilli

4 eggs, hard-boiled and roughly chopped

4 spring onions (scallions), finely chopped

1 tablespoon chopped dill

1 tablespoon lemon juice

115 g (4 oz) butter

3 teaspoons madras curry powder

50 g ($^1/_3$ cup) plain (all-purpose) flour

375 ml (1$^1/_2$ cups) milk

375 ml (1$^1/_2$ cups) cream

175 g (6 oz) whole-egg mayonnaise

3 x 210 g (7$^1/_2$ oz) cans tuna, drained

160 g (2 cups) fresh white breadcrumbs

1 garlic clove, crushed

1 tablespoon finely chopped flat-leaf (Italian) parsley

2 tablespoons grated Parmesan cheese

1   Preheat the oven to 180°C (350°F/Gas 4). Cook the pasta in a large saucepan of rapidly boiling salted water until al dente. Drain well. Lightly grease a 2 litre (8 cup) ovenproof dish. Combine the egg, spring onion, dill and lemon juice and season.

2   Melt 60 g (2$^1/_4$ oz) of the butter in a saucepan, add the curry powder and cook for 30 seconds. Stir in the flour and cook for 1 minute, or until foaming. Remove from the heat, gradually stir in the milk and cream, then return to low heat and stir constantly until the sauce boils and thickens. Reduce to a simmer for 2 minutes, then stir in the mayonnaise. Combine the sauce, cooked pasta, tuna and egg mixture and spoon into the prepared dish.

3   Melt the remaining butter in a frying pan, add the breadcrumbs and garlic and cook, stirring, for 1 minute, or until the breadcrumbs are golden and coated in butter. Stir in the parsley and grated Parmesan and then sprinkle over the tuna mixture. Bake for 15–20 minutes, or until golden and heated through.

INGREDIENTS

415 g (2 cups) orzo (rice-shaped pasta)
60 g (2$^1/_4$ oz) butter
6 spring onions (scallions), chopped
450 g (1 lb) English spinach, stems removed, rinsed well and chopped
2 tablespoons plain (all-purpose) flour
1.25 litres (5 cups) milk
250 g (9 oz) kefalotyri cheese, grated (see Note)
250 g (9 oz) marinated feta cheese, well drained
3 tablespoons chopped dill

1 Preheat the oven to 190°C (375°F/Gas 5). Cook the pasta in a large saucepan of boiling salted water until al dente. Drain well, then return to the pan. Heat 20 g ($^3/_4$ oz) of the butter in a large saucepan over high heat and cook the spring onion for 30 seconds. Add the spinach and stir for 1 minute. Season and stir into the orzo.

2 Put the remaining butter in the pan in which the spinach was cooked. Melt over low heat, then stir in the flour and cook for 1 minute, or until pale and foaming. Remove from the heat and gradually stir in the milk. Return to the heat and stir constantly for 5 minutes, or until the sauce boils and thickens. Add two-thirds of the kefalotyri and all of the feta and stir for 2 minutes, or until melted and well mixed. Remove from the heat and stir in the dill.

3 Combine the pasta mixture with the cheese sauce, season and pour into a greased 2.5 litre (10 cup) ovenproof ceramic dish. Sprinkle the remaining cheese over the top and bake for 15 minutes, or until golden.

NOTE Kefalotyri is a hard Greek sheep's or goat's milk cheese. Parmesan or pecorino cheese can be substituted.

500 g (1 lb 2 oz) penne rigate

80 ml ($^1/_3$ cup) extra virgin olive oil

4 garlic cloves, crushed

4 anchovy fillets, finely chopped

2 small red chillies, seeded and finely chopped

6 large, vine-ripened tomatoes, peeled, seeded and diced

80 ml ($^1/_3$ cup) white wine

1 tablespoon tomato paste (purée)

2 teaspoons sugar

2 tablespoons finely chopped flat-leaf (Italian) parsley

3 tablespoons shredded basil

1   Cook the pasta in a saucepan of boiling salted water until al dente. Drain well.

2   Meanwhile, heat the oil in a frying pan and cook the garlic for 30 seconds. Stir in the anchovy and chilli and cook for a further 30 seconds. Add the tomato and cook for 2 minutes over high heat. Add the wine, tomato paste and sugar and simmer, covered, for 10 minutes, or until thickened.

3   Toss the tomato sauce through the pasta with the herbs. Season and serve with grated Parmesan, if desired.

PASTA WITH TOMATO AND BASIL SAUCE

INGREDIENTS

2 tablespoons olive oil
500 g (1 lb 2 oz) button mushrooms, sliced
2 garlic cloves, crushed
2 teaspoons chopped marjoram
125 ml ($^1/_2$ cup) dry white wine
80 ml ($^1/_3$ cup) cream
375 g (13 oz) penne
1 tablespoon lemon juice
1 teaspoon finely grated lemon zest
2 tablespoons chopped parsley
50 g ($^1/_2$ cup) grated Parmesan cheese

1   Heat the oil in a large heavy-based frying pan over high heat. Add the mushrooms and cook for 3 minutes, stirring constantly to prevent the mushrooms from burning. Add the garlic and marjoram and cook for a further 2 minutes.

2   Add the white wine to the pan, reduce the heat and simmer for 5 minutes, or until nearly all the liquid has evaporated. Stir in the cream and cook over low heat for 5 minutes, or until the sauce has thickened.

3   Meanwhile, cook the penne in a large saucepan of boiling salted water until al dente. Drain.

4   Add the lemon juice, zest, parsley and half the Parmesan to the sauce. Season to taste with salt and freshly ground black pepper. Toss the penne through the sauce and sprinkle with the remaining Parmesan.

INGREDIENTS

125 ml ($^1/_2$ cup) olive oil
100 g ($3^1/_2$ oz) capers, patted dry
500 g (1 lb 2 oz) salmon fillets, skinned
625 g (1 lb 6 oz) ricotta agnolotti
150 g ($5^1/_2$ oz) butter
$1^1/_2$ teaspoons grated lemon zest
2 tablespoons lemon juice
3 tablespoons chopped parsley

1   Heat half the oil in a small frying pan and cook the capers over high heat for 3–4 minutes, or until golden and crispy. Drain on paper towels.

2   Season the salmon on both sides with salt and pepper. Heat the remaining oil in a non-stick frying pan and cook the salmon for 2–3 minutes each side, or until just cooked through but still pink in the centre. Remove from the pan and keep warm. Gently break into flakes with your fingers, being careful to remove any bones.

3   Cook the pasta in a large saucepan of boiling salted water until al dente. Drain and return to the pan to keep warm. Heat the butter in a frying pan over low heat for 5 minutes, or until golden. Add the lemon zest, lemon juice and parsley. Top the pasta with the flaked salmon and pour on the brown butter. Scatter with the capers and serve immediately.

INGREDIENTS

400 g (14 oz) dried egg tagliatelle
1 tablespoon olive oil
3 garlic cloves, finely chopped
20 medium raw prawns (shrimp), peeled and deveined, with tails intact
550 g (1 lb 4 oz) Roma (plum) tomatoes, diced
2 tablespoons thinly sliced basil
125 ml ($^1/_2$ cup) white wine
80 ml ($^1/_3$ cup) cream
basil leaves, to garnish

1   Cook the pasta in a large saucepan of boiling salted water until al dente. Drain and keep warm, reserving 2 tablespoons of the cooking water.

2   Meanwhile, heat the oil and garlic in a large frying pan over low heat for 1–2 minutes. Increase the heat to medium, add the prawns and cook for 3–5 minutes, stirring frequently until cooked. Remove the prawns and keep warm.

3   Add the tomato and sliced basil and stir for 3 minutes, or until the tomato is soft. Pour in the wine and cream, bring to the boil and simmer for 2 minutes.

4   Purée the sauce in a blender, return to the pan, then add the reserved pasta water and bring to a simmer. Stir in the prawns until heated through. Toss through the pasta and serve garnished with the basil leaves.

350 g (12 oz) fresh tagliatelle

3 garlic cloves, crushed

1 teaspoon finely grated lemon zest

80 ml ($^1/_3$ cup) extra virgin olive oil

500 g (1 lb 2 oz) tuna, cut into 1.5 cm ($^5/_8$ inch) cubes

200 g (7 oz) rocket (arugula) leaves, washed, dried and roughly chopped

4 tablespoons baby capers in salt, rinsed and squeezed dry

60 ml ($^1/_4$ cup) lemon juice

2 tablespoons finely chopped flat-leaf (Italian) parsley

1 Cook the pasta in a saucepan of boiling salted water until al dente.

2 Meanwhile, put the garlic, lemon zest and 1 tablespoon of the oil in a bowl with the tuna and gently mix. Season.

3 Heat a frying pan over high heat and sear the tuna for 30 seconds on each side. Add the rocket and capers and gently stir for 1 minute, or until the rocket has just wilted. Pour in the lemon juice and then remove from the heat.

4 Add the remaining oil to the hot pasta along with the tuna mixture and parsley. Season to taste and gently toss. Serve immediately.

TAGLIATELLE WITH TUNA, CAPERS AND ROCKET

PASTA CARBONARA

400 g (14 oz) penne
1 tablespoon olive oil
200 g (7 oz) piece pancetta or bacon, cut into long thin strips
6 egg yolks
185 ml ($^3/_4$ cup) thick (double/heavy) cream
75 g ($^3/_4$ cup) grated Parmesan cheese

1 Cook the pasta in a saucepan of boiling salted water until al dente.

2 Meanwhile, heat the oil in a frying pan and cook the pancetta over high heat for 6 minutes, or until crisp and golden. Remove with a slotted spoon and drain on paper towels.

3 Beat the egg yolks, cream and the Parmesan together in a bowl and season generously. Return the freshly cooked and drained pasta to its saucepan and pour the egg mixture over the pasta, tossing gently. Add the pancetta, then return the pan to very low heat and cook for 30–60 seconds, or until the sauce thickens and coats the pasta. Season with pepper and serve immediately.

NOTE Be careful not to cook the pasta over high heat once you have added the egg mixture, or the sauce risks being scrambled by the heat.

INGREDIENTS

120 g (4 oz) broad beans, fresh or frozen
150 g (5½ oz) asparagus, cut into short lengths
350 g (12 oz) fresh tagliatelle
100 g (3½ oz) green beans, cut into short lengths
120 g (¾ cup) peas, fresh or frozen
30 g (1 oz) butter
1 small fennel bulb, thinly sliced
375 ml (1½ cups) thick (double/heavy) cream
2 tablespoons grated Parmesan cheese, plus extra, to serve

1 Bring a large saucepan of water to the boil. Add 1 teaspoon of salt, the broad beans and asparagus and simmer for 3 minutes.

2 Remove the vegetables with a slotted spoon and set them aside. Add the tagliatelle to the saucepan and, when it has softened, stir in the beans and the peas (if you're using frozen peas, add them a few minutes later). Cook for about 4 minutes, or until the pasta is al dente.

3 Meanwhile, heat the butter in a large frying pan. Add the fennel and cook over moderately low heat without colouring for 5 minutes. Add the cream, season with salt and pepper and cook at a low simmer.

4 Peel the skins from the broad beans. Drain the pasta, green beans and peas and add them to the frying pan. Add 2 tablespoons of Parmesan and the broad beans and asparagus. Toss lightly to coat. Serve immediately with extra Parmesan.

INGREDIENTS

Meatballs

2 slices white bread, crusts removed

60 ml ($^1/_4$ cup) milk

500 g (1 lb 2 oz) minced (ground) pork and veal (see note)

1 small onion, finely chopped

2 garlic cloves, finely chopped

3 tablespoons finely chopped flat-leaf (Italian) parsley

2 teaspoons finely grated lemon zest

1 egg, lightly beaten

50 g ($^1/_2$ cup) grated Parmesan cheese

plain (all-purpose) flour, to coat

2 tablespoons olive oil

125 ml ($^1/_2$ cup) white wine

2 x 400 g (14 oz) cans chopped tomatoes

1 tablespoon tomato paste (purée)

1 teaspoon caster (superfine) sugar

$^1/_2$ teaspoon dried oregano

500 g (1 lb 2 oz) penne rigate (penne with ridges)

oregano leaves, to garnish

1   To make the meatballs, soak the bread in the milk for 5 minutes, then squeeze out any moisture. Put the bread, mince, onion, garlic, parsley, zest, egg and Parmesan in a bowl, season and mix well with your hands.

2   Shape into walnut-size balls using damp hands, and roll lightly in the flour. Heat the oil in a large deep frying pan and cook the meatballs in batches over medium heat, turning frequently, for 10 minutes, or until brown all over. Remove with a slotted spoon and drain on paper towels.

3   Pour the wine into the same frying pan and boil over medium heat for 2–3 minutes, or until it evaporates a little. Add the tomato, tomato paste, sugar and dried oregano. Reduce the heat, then simmer for 20 minutes to thicken the sauce. Add the meatballs and simmer for 10 minutes. Meanwhile, cook the pasta in a saucepan of boiling salted water until al dente.

4   To serve, divide the hot pasta among six serving plates and spoon some meatballs and sauce over the top of each. Garnish with the oregano.

Use minced beef instead of the pork and veal, if you prefer.

INGREDIENTS

400 g (14 oz) spaghettini (thin spaghetti)
125 ml ($^1/_2$ cup) olive oil
4 garlic cloves, finely chopped
10 anchovy fillets, chopped
1 tablespoon baby capers, rinsed and squeezed dry
1 teaspoon chilli flakes
2 tablespoons lemon juice
2 teaspoons finely grated lemon zest
3 tablespoons chopped parsley
3 tablespoons chopped basil leaves
3 tablespoons chopped mint
50 g ($^1/_2$ cup) coarsely grated Parmesan cheese, plus extra, to serve
extra virgin olive oil, to drizzle

1   Cook the pasta in a saucepan of boiling salted water until al dente.

2   Heat the oil in a frying pan and cook the garlic over medium heat for 2–3 minutes, or until starting to brown. Add the anchovies, capers and chilli and cook for 1 minute.

3   Add the hot pasta to the pan with the lemon juice, zest, parsley, basil, mint and Parmesan. Season with salt and pepper and toss together well.

4   To serve, drizzle with a little extra oil and sprinkle with Parmesan.

PASTA WITH GRILLED CAPSICUM

6 large red capsicums (peppers), halved
400 g (14 oz) pasta gnocchi (see note)
2 tablespoons olive oil
1 onion, thinly sliced
3 garlic cloves, finely chopped
2 tablespoons shredded basil leaves
whole basil leaves, to garnish
shaved Parmesan cheese, to serve

1 Cut the capsicums into large flattish pieces. Cook, skin side up, under a hot grill (broiler) until the skin blackens and blisters. Place in a plastic bag and leave to cool, then peel the skin.

2 Cook the pasta in a saucepan of boiling salted water until al dente. Meanwhile, heat the oil in a large frying pan, add the onion and garlic and cook over medium heat for 5 minutes, or until soft. Cut one capsicum into thin strips and add to the onion mixture.

3 Chop the remaining capsicum, then purée in a food processor until smooth. Add to the onion mixture and cook over low heat for 5 minutes, or until warmed through.

4 Toss the sauce through the hot pasta. Season, then stir in the shredded basil. Garnish with the basil leaves and serve with the Parmesan.

INGREDIENTS

1 kg (2 lb 4 oz) baby clams (vongole)
375 g (13 oz) spaghetti
125 ml ($^1/_2$ cup) virgin olive oil
40 g (1$^1/_2$ oz) butter
1 small onion, very finely chopped
6 large garlic cloves, finely chopped
125 ml ($^1/_2$ cup) dry white wine
1 small red chilli, seeded and finely chopped
15 g ($^1/_2$ cup) chopped flat-leaf (Italian) parsley

1   Scrub the clams with a small stiff brush to remove any grit, discarding any that are open or cracked. Then soak and rinse the clams in several changes of water over an hour or so until the water is clean and free of grit. Drain and set aside.

2   Cook the pasta in a saucepan of boiling salted water until al dente.

3   Heat the oil and 1 tablespoon of the butter in a large saucepan over medium heat. Add the onion and half the garlic and cook for 10 minutes, or until lightly golden — ensure the garlic doesn't start to burn. Add the wine and cook for 2 minutes. Then add the clams, chilli and the remaining butter and garlic and cook, covered, for 8 minutes, shaking regularly, until the clams pop open — discard any that are still closed.

4   Stir in the parsley and season. Add the hot pasta and toss well.

PENNE ALL'ARRABBIATA

2 tablespoons olive oil
2 large garlic cloves, thinly sliced
1–2 medium-sized dried chillies
2 x 400 g (14 oz) cans tomatoes
400 g (14 oz) penne or rigatoni
1 basil sprig, torn into pieces

1 Heat the olive oil in a saucepan and add the garlic and chillies. Cook over low heat until the garlic is light golden brown. Turn the chillies over during cooking so both sides get a chance to infuse in the oil and turn slightly nutty in flavour. Add the tomatoes and season with salt. Cook gently, breaking up the tomatoes with a wooden spoon, for 20–30 minutes, or until the sauce is rich and thick.

2 Meanwhile, cook the pasta in a large saucepan of boiling salted water until al dente. Drain.

3 Add the basil to the sauce and season just before serving, tossed with the pasta. If you prefer a hotter sauce, break open the chilli to release the seeds.

INGREDIENTS

500 g (1 lb 2 oz) spaghetti
1 tablespoon olive oil
1 onion, finely chopped
3 garlic cloves, finely chopped
2 x 400 g (14 oz) cans chopped tomatoes
2 tablespoons tomato paste (purée)
170 ml ($^2/_3$ cup) dry white wine
2 teaspoons soft brown sugar
1 teaspoon finely grated lemon zest
2 tablespoons torn basil leaves, plus extra, to garnish
2 tablespoons finely chopped flat-leaf (Italian) parsley
12 medium raw prawns (shrimp), peeled and deveined, with tails intact
8 black mussels, scrubbed and beards removed
8 large white scallops, without roe
2 small squid tubes, cleaned and cut into 1 cm ($^1/_2$ inch) rings

1   Cook the pasta in a saucepan of boiling salted water until al dente.

2   Meanwhile, heat the oil in a large saucepan, add the onion and cook over medium heat for 5–8 minutes, or until golden. Add the garlic, tomato, tomato paste, wine, sugar, lemon zest, 1 tablespoon of the basil, parsley and 250 ml (1 cup) water. Cook, stirring occasionally, for 1 hour, or until the sauce is reduced and thickened. Season.

3   Add the prawns and mussels and cook for 1 minute, then add the scallops and cook for 2 minutes. Stir in the squid and cook for 1 minute more, or until all the seafood is cooked through and tender.

4   Add the hot pasta to the sauce with the remaining basil and toss together until well combined. Serve.

RAVIOLI WITH PRAWNS AND CREAMY LIME SAUCE

50 g (1³/₄ oz) butter

4 garlic cloves, crushed

750 g (1 lb 10 oz) medium raw prawns (shrimp), peeled and deveined

1¹/₂ tablespoons plain (all-purpose) flour

375 ml (1¹/₂ cups) fish stock

500 ml (2 cups) cream

5 makrut (kaffir) lime leaves, shredded

650 g (1 lb 7 oz) seafood ravioli (see note)

3 teaspoons fish sauce

1 Melt the butter in a large deep frying pan and cook the garlic over medium heat for 1 minute. Add the prawns and cook for 3–4 minutes, or until they turn pink and are cooked through. Remove from the pan, leaving any juices in the pan. Add the flour and stir for 1 minute, or until lightly golden. Gradually stir in the stock, then add the cream and lime leaves. Reduce the heat and simmer for 10 minutes, or until slightly thickened.

2 Meanwhile, cook the pasta in a large saucepan of boiling salted water until al dente. Drain.

3 Stir the fish sauce through the cream sauce, add the prawns and stir until warmed through. Divide the pasta among four warm serving plates and spoon on the prawns and sauce. Season with salt and cracked black pepper and serve.

NOTE Seafood ravioli is available from speciality pasta shops, but if it is unavailable you can use ricotta ravioli instead — the flavours work well.

500 g (1 lb 2 oz) ham and cheese tortellini
60 g (2^1/$_4$ oz) butter
100 g (1 cup) walnuts, chopped
100 g (^{2}/$_3$ cup) pine nuts
2 tablespoons finely chopped flat-leaf (Italian) parsley
2 teaspoons chopped thyme
60 g (^{1}/$_4$ cup) ricotta cheese
60 ml (^{1}/$_4$ cup) thick (double/heavy) cream

1   Cook the pasta in a large saucepan of boiling water until al dente. Drain and return to the pan.

2   Meanwhile, heat the butter in a frying pan over medium heat until foaming. Add the walnuts and pine nuts and stir for 5 minutes, or until golden brown. Add the parsley and thyme and season to taste.

3   Beat the ricotta and cream together. Add the nutty sauce to the pasta and toss. Divide among serving bowls and top with the ricotta cream.

TAGLIATELLE WITH PRAWNS AND LEEK IN SAFFRON CREAM

40 g (1¹/₂ oz) butter
1 small leek, julienned
4 garlic cloves, finely chopped
pinch of saffron threads
125 ml (¹/₂ cup) dry vermouth
250 ml (1 cup) fish stock
300 ml (10¹/₂ fl oz) thick (double/heavy) cream
400 g (14 oz) fresh tagliatelle or any long, flat pasta
24 medium raw prawns (shrimp), peeled and deveined, with tails intact
1 tablespoon lemon juice
1 tablespoon finely chopped chervil, plus extra, to garnish

1 Melt the butter in a saucepan over medium heat, add the leek and garlic and cook for 5 minutes, or until the leek is soft and translucent. Add the saffron, vermouth and fish stock and bring to the boil, skimming off any scum that rises to the surface. Reduce the heat to low and simmer for 10 minutes, or until the sauce has reduced by half. Pour in the cream and simmer for 15 minutes, or until the sauce has thickened and reduced by about a third.

2 Meanwhile, cook the pasta in a saucepan of boiling salted water until al dente.

3 Add the prawns to the sauce and simmer for 2–3 minutes, or until cooked through. Remove from the heat and stir in the lemon juice and chervil. Season well, then toss through the hot pasta. Serve immediately, garnished with a little extra chervil, if desired.

NOTE This creamy pasta is very rich and more suitable as a starter than a main course.

INGREDIENTS

2 tablespoons olive oil
200 g (7 oz) pancetta, thinly sliced
1 red onion, finely chopped
2 garlic cloves, finely chopped
1 teaspoon chilli flakes
2 teaspoons finely chopped rosemary
2 x 400 g (14 oz) cans chopped tomatoes
500 g (1 lb 2 oz) bucatini or spaghetti
15 g ($^1/_2$ cup) chopped flat-leaf (Italian) parsley

1   Heat the oil in a frying pan and cook the pancetta over medium heat for 6–8 minutes, or until crisp. Add the onion, garlic, chilli flakes and chopped rosemary and cook for 4–5 minutes more, or until the onion has softened.

2   Add the tomato to the pan, season with salt and pepper, and bring to the boil. Reduce the heat to low and simmer for 20 minutes, or until the sauce is reduced and very thick.

3   Meanwhile, cook the pasta in a large saucepan of boiling salted water until al dente.

4   Toss the sauce with the hot pasta and parsley, then serve.

INGREDIENTS

1 kg (2 lb 4 oz) jap pumpkin, cut into 2 cm ($^3/_4$ inch) cubes
600 g (1 lb 5 oz) veal tortellini
100 g ($3^1/_2$ oz) butter
3 garlic cloves, crushed
80 g ($^1/_2$ cup) pine nuts
45 g ($^3/_4$ cup) firmly packed shredded basil
200 g (7 oz) feta cheese, crumbled

1   Preheat the oven to 220°C (425°F/Gas 7). Line a baking tray with baking paper. Place the pumpkin on the prepared tray and season well with salt and cracked black pepper. Bake for 30 minutes, or until tender.

2   Meanwhile, cook the pasta in a large saucepan of boiling salted water until al dente. Drain and return to the pan.

3   Heat the butter over medium heat in a small frying pan until foaming. Add the garlic and pine nuts and cook for 3–5 minutes, or until the nuts are starting to turn golden. Remove from the heat and add the basil. Toss the basil butter, pumpkin and feta through the cooked pasta and serve.

INGREDIENTS

30 g (1 oz) butter
4 rashers bacon, diced
2 garlic cloves, finely chopped
300 g (10^1/$_2$ oz) Swiss brown or button mushrooms, sliced
60 ml (^{1}/$_4$ cup) dry white wine
375 ml (1^1/$_2$ cups) cream
1 teaspoon chopped thyme
500 g (1 lb 2 oz) veal tortellini
50 g (^{1}/$_2$ cup) grated Parmesan cheese
1 tablespoon chopped flat-leaf (Italian) parsley

1 Melt the butter in a large frying pan, add the bacon and cook over medium heat for 5 minutes, or until crisp. Add the garlic and cook for 2 minutes, then add the mushrooms, cooking for a further 8 minutes, or until softened.

2 Stir in the wine and cream and add the thyme and bring to the boil. Reduce the heat to low and simmer for 10 minutes, or until the sauce has thickened. Meanwhile, cook the pasta in a large saucepan of boiling salted water until al dente

3 Combine the sauce with the hot pasta, Parmesan and parsley. Season to taste and serve immediately.

SPAGHETTINI WITH SQUID IN BLACK INK

1 kg (2 lb 4 oz) medium squid
2 tablespoons olive oil
1 onion, finely chopped
6 garlic cloves, finely chopped
1 bay leaf
1 small red chilli, seeded and thinly sliced
80 ml ($^1/_3$ cup) white wine
80 ml ($^1/_3$ cup) dry vermouth
250 ml (1 cup) fish stock
60 g ($^1/_4$ cup) tomato paste (purée)
500 ml (2 cups) tomato passata
15 g ($^1/_2$ oz) squid ink
500 g (1 lb 2 oz) spaghettini
$^1/_2$ teaspoon Pernod (optional)
4 tablespoons chopped flat-leaf (Italian) parsley
1 garlic clove, extra, crushed

1 To clean the squid, pull the tentacles away from the hood (the intestines should come away at the same time). Remove the intestines by cutting under the eyes, and remove the beak by using your fingers to push up the centre. Pull out the transparent quill from inside the body. Remove any white membrane. Cut the squid into thin slices.

2 Heat the oil in a saucepan over medium heat. Add the onion and cook until lightly golden. Add the garlic, bay leaf and chilli and cook for 2 minutes, or until the garlic is lightly golden. Stir in the wine, vermouth, stock, tomato paste, passata and 250 ml (1 cup) water, then increase the heat to high and bring to the boil. Reduce to a simmer and cook for 45 minutes, or until the liquid has reduced by half. Add the squid ink and cook for 2 minutes, or until the sauce is evenly black and glossy. Meanwhile, cook the pasta in a large saucepan of boiling salted water until al dente.

3 Add the squid rings and Pernod, stir well, then cook for 4–5 minutes, or until they turn opaque and are cooked through. Stir in the parsley and the extra garlic and season. Toss through the hot pasta and serve immediately.

INGREDIENTS

2 tablespoons olive oil

2 garlic cloves, finely chopped

1 large onion, finely chopped

1 carrot, finely chopped

1 celery stalk, finely chopped

50 g (1³/₄ oz) pancetta or bacon, finely chopped

500 g (1 lb 2 oz) minced (ground) beef

500 ml (2 cups) beef stock

375 ml (1¹/₂ cups) red wine

2 x 400 g (14 oz) cans chopped tomatoes

2 tablespoons tomato paste (purée)

1 teaspoon sugar

500 g (1 lb 2 oz) fresh tagliatelle (see note)

shaved Parmesan cheese, to serve

1   Heat the oil in a large deep saucepan. Add the garlic, onion, carrot, celery and pancetta and cook, stirring, over medium heat for about 5 minutes, or until softened.

2   Add the mince and break up any lumps with the back of a spoon, stirring until just browned. Add the stock, red wine, tomatoes, tomato paste and sugar. Bring to the boil, then reduce the heat to very low and simmer, covered, stirring occasionally, for 1¹/₂ hours. Remove the lid and simmer, stirring occasionally, for a further 1¹/₂ hours. Season to taste with salt and freshly ground pepper. While the meat is cooking, cook the pasta in a saucepan of boiling salted water until al dente.

3   To serve, spoon the sauce over the hot pasta and sprinkle with some of the shaved Parmesan.

NOTE   Traditionally, bolognese was served with tagliatelle, but now we tend to serve it with spaghetti.

SPAGHETTI PUTTANESCA

400 g (14 oz) spaghetti
2 tablespoons olive oil
1 onion, finely chopped
2 garlic cloves, finely sliced
1 small red chilli, cored, seeded and sliced
6 anchovy fillets, finely chopped
400 g (14 oz) canned chopped tomatoes
1 tablespoon fresh oregano, finely chopped
16 black olives, halved and pitted
2 tablespoons baby capers
a handful basil leaves

1 Cook the spaghetti in a large saucepan of boiling salted water until al dente, stirring once or twice to make sure the pieces are not stuck together. The cooking time will vary depending on the brand of spaghetti. Check the pasta occasionally as it cooks because the time given on packet instructions is often too long by a minute or two.

2 Heat the olive oil in a large saucepan and add the onion, garlic and chilli. Gently fry for about 8 minutes, or until the onion is soft. Add the anchovies and cook for another minute. Add the tomato, oregano, olive halves and capers and bring to the boil. Reduce the heat, season with salt and pepper, and leave the sauce to simmer for 3 minutes.

3 Drain the spaghetti and add it to the sauce. Toss together well so that the pasta is coated in the sauce. Scatter the basil over the top and serve.

All our recipes are thoroughly tested in a specially developed test kitchen. Standard metric measuring cups and spoons are used in the development of our recipes. All cup and spoon measurements are level. We have used 60 g (2¼ oz/Grade 3) eggs in all recipes. Sizes of cans vary from manufacturer to manufacturer and between countries – use the can size closest to the one suggested in the recipe.

CONVERSION GUIDE

1 cup = 250 ml (9 fl oz)

1 teaspoon = 5 ml

1 Australian tablespoon = 20 ml (4 teaspoons)

1 UK/US tablespoon = 15 ml (3 teaspoons)

DRY MEASURES	LIQUID MEASURES	LINEAR MEASURES
30 g = 1 oz	30 ml = 1 fl oz	6 mm = ¼ inch
250 g = 9 oz	125 ml = 4 fl oz	1 cm = ½ inch
500 g = 1 lb 2 oz	250 ml = 9 fl oz	2.5 cm = 1 inch

CUP CONVERSIONS – DRY INGREDIENTS

1 cup almonds, slivered whole = 125 g (4½ oz)

1 cup cheese, lightly packed processed cheddar = 155 g (5½ oz)

1 cup wheat flour = 125 g (4½ oz)

1 cup wholemeal flour = 140 g (5 oz)

1 cup minced (ground) meat = 250 g (9 oz)

1 cup pasta shapes = 125 g (4½ oz)

1 cup raisins = 170 g (6 oz)

1 cup rice, short grain, raw = 200 g (7 oz)

1 cup sesame seeds = 160 g (6 oz)

1 cup split peas = 250 g (9 oz)

INTERNATIONAL GLOSSARY

capsicum	sweet bell pepper
chick pea	garbanzo bean
chilli	chile, chili pepper
cornflour	cornstarch
eggplant	aubergine
spring onion	scallion
zucchini	courgette
plain flour	all-purpose flour
prawns	shrimp
minced meat	ground meat

Where temperature ranges are indicated, the lower figure applies to gas ovens, the higher to electric ovens. This allows for the fact that the flame in gas ovens generates a drier heat, which effectively cooks food faster than the moister heat of an electric oven, even if the temperature setting is the same.

	°C	°F	GAS MARK
Very slow	120	250	½
Slow	150	300	2
Mod slow	160	325	3
Moderate	180	350	4
Mod hot	190(g)–210(e)	375–425	5
Hot	200(g)–240(e)	400–475	6
Very hot	230(g)–260(e)	450–525	8

INDEX

Published in 2006 by Bay Books,
an imprint of Murdoch Books Pty Limited.

ISBN 1-74045-940-7
978-1-74045-940-2

Printed by Sing Cheong Printing Company Ltd.
Printed in China.